PARENTING IN THE 21ST CENTURY:
A HORROR STORY

A guide for surviving your children from birth until they fly the coop

Barbara Woster

Copyright © 2018 Barbara Woster
All rights reserved.
ISBN—13:9781732843325
ISBN eBook—9781733660242

DEDICATION

Thanks to my family without whom this book (and all my others) would never have been written.

Thanks to my two youngest daughters for providing Mom with the graphics for this book. I know you both drew these as a joke, and I know how talented you are, but I love them.

Introduction

It generally begins with *"Can I ask you a question?"*

Whether the question is being asked by my own adult kids, young parents; or by the parents of my daycare kids, they all seem to think I have the answers to life's greatest mystery—children. What in the name of all that's holy would give them the impression that I even know what I'm talking about? What makes someone qualified to answer questions posed to them about the littlest of our species.

Well, let's see if I'm qualified. First, I own and operate a state-registered daycare facility, and work with the smallest of the small daily. Does that make me qualified? Not really, but it helps.

Next, I have a bachelor's degree in Elementary Education from Grand Canyon University; and obtained a master's degree in Early Childhood Development from Concordia University. Graduated Summa Cum Laude. So, does that make me qualified? Another notch in the qualifications checklist, but still doesn't make me fully qualified. After all, I have seen a lot of books written by child psychologists, and others, that I wouldn't touch with the proverbial 10-foot pole, despite having multiple degrees. Why? Well, here's what makes someone truly qualified…

Because, unless they have raised children, they shouldn't be offering advice on how to rear them. Do I have children? Four children, four stepchildren, and seven grandchildren (at the time this book was written). However, had those children turned out to be delinquents…well, I'd still be qualified, because you can learn from my mistakes. Fortunately, my children are all successful in life; productive, contributing members of society, but it was a long, difficult road getting them there. So, in short, had I not made the thousands of mistakes that young or new parents make; had I not learned from those mistakes and obtained the education needed to continue learning, I would not be in a position to write this book.

My husband said something recently that is very apropos to raising children. He said that it takes years to glean the lessons learned from prior difficult circumstances. For parents, this is so true. It takes years of raising a child, going through Hell (and the joys), before we can begin to comprehend what we're doing and how to begin doing it better, doing it right. I think that's one reason we turn to those "experts" who have been there and experienced children in all their glorious mischief—because we want to understand and comprehend *now*.

It takes wisdom to seek out advice from someone wiser; someone who's already been down a particular road. Perhaps, by reading this book, newer parents—or struggling parents—can glean knowledge to help them along the parental path. That's my hope, and why I wrote this book.

Oh—and a quick note—I will be using examples from real situations in my own life, the life of my children, my siblings, and other parents with whom I've had a lot of interaction. Moreover, many of the topics covered were generated from questions asked of me over the years.

All names in the examples and scenarios have been changed, of course.

PART 1: They don't come with receipts, so think carefully before giving up birth control

If you are contemplating having children, or are in the process of preparing for the birth of a child, there's a little something you've probably heard many times before—once you have a child, you can't give 'em back; so before I delve into the world of raising children, I thought it would be nice to pass on a few tips to those preparing to welcome their little darlings into the world, or considering having one at all.

Just a quick note before proceeding—I love children. I love their idiosyncrasies, their innocence, their propensity towards mischief, and the joy they bring to our lives; but I also know that they can cause mayhem, destruction, and misery to those ill-equipped to raise them; and that will last your entire lifetime.

This book is meant to be the voice of experience, to assist new parents and those contemplating children; as well as those who have already had children and are simply seeking advice on a specific age group.

They are not a cure all

I'll probably have a lot of readers thinking, *mind your own business*; however, if I didn't state this, I would be neglecting an essential element of planning a family. Children will not fix your marriage. In fact, they will only give you one more thing to fight about and fight over. If you're thinking of having a child because you think it will repair whatever damages your marriage has incurred, try marriage therapy instead. In the long run, the therapy will cost you far less than raising a child will and will do more to mend whatever's broken. There, that's my two cents worth.

Be on the same page

Think of this as having a game plan before a big game; or planning for the vacation of a lifetime. In fact, you'll want to sit down with your significant other and hold a serious discussion for contingencies when things go awry as well as evacuation plans...oh, wait! There are no evacuation plans. You're in this for the long haul, so when I say to be on the same page, you better believe I mean it; because if your children get one whiff of a notion that you and your spouse are divided on anything—whether that something is discipline, chores, or allowances—they are going to take advantage. Divide and conquer will take on a whole new meaning.

So, sit down and discuss every possible contingency and how you plan to handle it *as a couple*. Are one of you in support of assigning chores, while the other thinks chores equate to child slave labor? Does one of you think that discipline means a trip to the shed, and the other think that discipline means calmly explaining what the child did wrong? If you're that far divided, your child is going to conquer—with ease. This conversation will take time, so jot down things to discuss over a period of weeks, then come together to talk about them all. What are some of the areas of discussion that you and your spouse should come to terms on? Let's look at a few:

How to discipline: As mentioned above, you and your spouse need to decide what types of discipline will be used for different infractions; and there will be thousands of types of infractions. From sassing to back talking; from disobeying to fighting, you both will need to decide how you're going to handle things as they arise. Later, I'll discuss this more in detail.

To give chores or not: There really are people in this world who believe that young children should not be subjected to doing any type of work; that their little lives should be nothing but play, eat, and sleep. There are others who believe that children should begin doing little tasks the moment they can walk. You and your spouse need to discuss your individual viewpoints and work on the types of chores you're willing to dole out and the rewards/consequences associated.

Allowances for allowances: When I was young, my mother had a list of chores that my siblings and I were to complete each Saturday, for which we were paid ten cents each chore. Amazingly, it equated to precisely two dollars. That doesn't seem a lot, but when I was a child, that two dollars got us a movie ticket, popcorn, a drink, and candy with the leftovers. Knowing how much things cost today, calculating what you can afford to "pay" your child, and for what you'll provide money for are some good starting points for discussions on allowances.

Dating: Do you want your child to begin dating at fourteen and your spouse thinks they should wait until they're forty? Well, that's a bit extreme, but knowing where your spouse stands on dating will prevent disagreements in future; disagreements with which your child will use to divide and conquer. You may not think that this is important to discuss when the baby-to-be is still in the womb, or a future consideration, but it can cause contention and needs to be at least touched on before deciding to have a child.

Other areas of discussion may be as benign as play dates, sleepovers, when you'll allow them to start working or driving, ear/body piercings, tattoos, hair coloring, types of permitted clothing to wear…the list goes on. Knowing the others' viewpoints on child rearing will certainly assist in avoiding unpleasant surprises when that first disagreeable task arrives. Even something as simple as, "are you going to help me change diapers?" will prevent the eruption of World War III when that darling baby offers up his or her first bowel movement.

And for heaven's sakes above—don't assume or presume that you know your spouse so well that y'all will just mesh and raising your baby will be magical perfection (yeah, right). Oh, and if there's any doubt whatsoever on whether you and your spouse agree—wing it, fake it, do whatever it takes to present a united front. If necessary, just say, "Whatever your Mom says, goes" or "Your Dad said it, so therefore you follow it." Quite simply, make "we're a united front" your new mantra. If it needs discussing because you aren't quite ready to give carte blanche to your spouse, then take the discussion to a different room, away from your children. Don't let them see that you're not of a single mind or they will make your life a living Hell.

Zen will become your new best friend

If you aren't religious, you'll find it fast raising a child. "Oh, dear Lord", "God have mercy", and other charming—and not-so-charming—expletives will become a permanent part of your repertoire. So, when I say, *Zen will become your new best friend*, all I'm relaying is that it would be in your best interest to learn calming techniques *before* you start losing your calm.

Some popular methods in use for eons are yoga, Tai Chi, counting to ten (or a hundred); and—short of becoming a Buddhist—some nice meditation or breathing exercises. If you wonder why these relaxation methods are so popular, you won't wonder for long once you've lost your first month's sleep, or when your teenager goes ballistic because you asked them to change their booty shorts. For me, when dealing with the insanity of my children, I tend to take deep breaths and start counting, until I know I can address the insanity with calm rationale. It isn't always easy to accomplish, but just trying and making it a habit will prove beneficial and allow you to remain in charge of your home.

Learning calming techniques will also save your sanity (and reduce those wrinkles, gray hairs, and ulcers {not guaranteed}) as your child grows and you're faced with even more crying, temper tantrums, and back talking (yes, I promise to cover those charming traits a bit later). Not really the religious sort? Well then, become a teatotaler. There are some teas renowned for preserving one's sanity, or at least calming one's nerves, such as Chamomile.

While Alcohol might seem a perfect anti-stress option, try using it in moderation—or not at all. Your child is going to provide a *lifetime* of joy and pain, and you're going to need to remain lucid and upright to face the challenges ahead, as well as to enjoy the fun times. Am I against alcohol? No. However, I am against using it as a medication to combat the craziness of life. That is why I will always recommend non-mind-altering alternatives ahead of mind-numbing ones.

Raising a child is like erecting a building & playing professional athletics simultaneously

"Tag! You're it!"

Parents should have the mentality that they're a tag-team on a wrestling squad. Without communication, you're going to get pinned fast to the mat and are not going to be able to get up (children are stronger than they look).

On top of being amazing at sports—chasing, wrestling, and developing awesome plays to outwit them at every turn—you will also need to be superior at construction. Yes, I said construction.

In education, we refer to a child's developmental learning as scaffolding. Sounds construction-y, doesn't it? In reality, once that baby is born, you will begin constructing its life, and if you do not raise up a strong building—um, child—then he or she is going to topple the moment those hurricane-force winds hit (a.k.a. *life*).

In addition to rearing them with the proper strength to face all of life's challenges, you will also be, simultaneously, building a proper relationship with you and your spouse, beginning with a strong foundation of love and respect. Why is that important? Because *life* doesn't just assault individuals, it does its darndest to knock down families as well...and I think you can guess where this analogy is headed, so...ready, set, it's time to raise a child.

PART 2: How to discipline a child when gluing their butts to a chair isn't allowed.

The more popular questions I'm asked invariably relates to discipline. Many people hear the word discipline and automatically go on the defensive, fearing that it correlates with *abuse*. Had not morons over the centuries given people that impression, many would not fear it; rather they would embrace the true meaning: *Discipline* comes from *discipulus*, the Latin word for *pupil* (1)

Knowing the true meaning, however, doesn't make it any easier to swallow. It is, without a doubt, the hardest area of child rearing to come to terms with because it generally involves unpleasant emotions: anger, distress, sadness, and guilt. Still, without discipline, a child will not learn boundaries, respect, responsibility, acceptable behavior, socialization…the list goes on. Discipline is where child rearing begins; it's the heart of the building.

From the moment they toss that first toy out of their crib, you pick it up, and they toss it back out despite you telling them not to; to the moment they look at you and say, "I hate you!" because you grounded them for being disrespectful—

discipline will keep your building from toppling during the many storms that will hit your family in the years ahead.

What is discipline?

As mentioned above, *Discipline* comes from *discipulus*, the Latin word for *pupil*. However, this is not how it's been defined or used. In fact, the earliest known use of *discipline* appears to be punishment-related as it first was used in the 13th century to refer to chastisement of a religious nature, such as *self-flagellation* (2). Moreover, the dictionary defines *discipline* as "training that makes people more willing to obey or more able to control themselves, often in the form of rules and punishments, if these are broken, or the behaviour produced by this training" (3)

Well, all that sounds daunting and unpleasant. No wonder the idea of discipline generates such negative emotions. No wonder so many parents turn to permissive passivity—basically bailing on disciplining altogether. Yikes!

After disciplining my fair share of children and falling back on the true meaning as that of a "pupil", I developed my own definition of discipline: *There are positive and negative consequences to every action; that every action we take affects others; therefore, we must advance positive behaviors, teach good listening skills, and realize that there are rules that we must follow—legal and societal.* As parents, it's our job—nay, our duty—to instruct our child in a manner that will shape them into responsible, capable, productive adults. So, how exactly are we supposed to do this? While there is no magic pill we can just give to our child as they grow (I wish), there are techniques we can employ to make things go…well, while not precisely smooth, at least assist in creating less life-threatening waves. These next few techniques will work for children, no matter the age—if used *consistently*. And just for edification, I'll use *consistently* a lot in this book, because without consistency, you'll struggle more in rearing your child than needs be.

Successful parenting depends on consistency

That's the first key and primary to success *at all ages*. If you do not parent with consistency, children will become confused and as a result, less likely to rely on parents as a guide. What is consistency in discipline? Well, again, I sort of formulated my own definition: *It's following through with consequences—positive or negative—in an unwavering manner, maintaining penalties and rewards equal to the resulting positive or negative act.* Let's look at a quick couple of examples.

Johnny is twelve. His sister, Amy, is eight. Johnny gets upset with Amy and hits her. The first time the parent does nothing, just picks up Amy and coos in comfort. Johnny isn't disciplined. The next time Johnny hits Amy, his parent yells, "Don't do that again. It's mean!" Once again, Johnny hits Amy, so his parent smacks him on the head and shouts, "How do *you* like it!" Johnny—still not getting the message, does it again. His parent sends him to his room and takes away his television. Yet, again, Johnny (whose brain hasn't developed yet and requires a lot of work) smacks his sister, so his parent threatens to call the police to report him for child abuse.

Okay, whew, let's stop there because this is getting nuts. First, Johnny's parents had no pre-determined course of action laid out in their mind over how to handle situations as they arise. They simply reacted at that moment—and poorly. Each time, the aggravation resulted in a more and more unlikely scenario and throughout was both inconsistent and disproportionate to Johnny's conduct. We'll discuss a better way to handle Johnny's behavior momentarily.

On the flip side, positive behavior needs consistency also. You can't offer an ice cream for putting away toys one day and then renege the next time. You can't tell a child that they'll get a dollar for every A on their report card one semester and then say, "Oh, well, this semester it's zero." Just as negative consequences need to be thought out carefully, so do positive consequences.

Remember that game plan we discussed in the introduction? Well positive, consistent consequences need to be among the top discussions prior to bringing a child into the world.

We all have probably heard that children go through one of several different abusive phases—biting, pulling hair, or hitting—and if you weren't aware of that, you are now; and if you don't think your child will do any of these, you're either naïve or in denial. Of course, there are those exceptions to every rule. Maybe there is a child out there who'll never hit, pull hair, or bite; and there may be some that will do all three. I have yet to meet or work with a child who hasn't done one or another. Knowing this in advance, you can sit down with your spouse to formulate what actions you'll take, consistently and calmly, should any or all the above take place. You won't be able to discuss and plan for every scenario, but there are certain base tactics that can be used as a template for every scenario.

For example, there's the ever-popular *time out*. Many state agencies however frown on this because it simply generates anger and does nothing in offering a resolution. However, it is possible to make *time out* work in our favor; for it to become a template, if used in conjunction with other measures.

First, *time out* should be an uncomfortable chair in a corner; not on the couch where they can play, or in their room where they are free to roam. I have a hard chair that sits in a corner of my living room. So then let's consider how to effectively use *time out*.

If we combine *time out* with a short discussion—and I did say short discussion, since long-winded monologues will fall on deaf ears—on why it is improper behavior and follow up with a consequence (and remember it needs to be equal to the offense), then we have a good formula that can be used throughout childhood, no matter the offense: time out, short discussion, consequence. Even toddlers can be talked to and given consequences, and most definitely teenagers can. As a child moves into their teenage years, the *time out* chair can be removed from the template. By then we should be able to just sit down with them, hold a civil conversation and give an appropriate consequence.

I would like to interject here that consequences should not be that which interferes with a child's education or attitude towards a needed skill. For instance, we should not make a child write sentences or essays. This used to be a good disciplinary ploy because it was meant to make the consequence sink in (writing sentences); or as a method for "thinking" about what was done (writing an essay). So, if there are supposed positive outcomes surrounding this type of consequence, why avoid it? Because if we use writing as a negative consequence, then it will be viewed negatively in all instances, such as when a child is in school and is asked to write an expository essay. Well, if they are taught that writing is a negative consequence to an action, they are going to approach educational writing in a negative light. I think it would be preferred that we encourage writing, especially today when keyboards rein.

Also, we should not "punish" a child by removing educational learning tools, such as reading. If we refuse to read to a child because they were naughty, or if we tell them that their reading privileges are removed along with computer time…well, we're removing an essential tool in their growth. If we remove the computer and television, and reading is all that's left to them, think of the benefits to that consequence: enhanced reading skills, better grammar, and spelling skills, etc.

As for consequences not associated with a child's education, we need to ensure they are rational and doable. We can't threaten to kill them, because that isn't rational nor doable, and falls beneath the "extreme" category, which we'll discuss later. Moreover, we need to ensure that the consequence is instant, not drawn out. In other words, we aren't to keep punishing a child for an infraction repeatedly just because we're still irritated over what they did. The child forgets what they did quickly, so we need to put it behind us equally quick. So, sit them down, quickly explain the infraction, have a consequence that is appropriate to the behavior (and age) *and* short (half hour to an hour max, depending on age and severity).

So, let's look at Johnny's propensity to whack at his sister consistently (I told you we'd get back to this ☺). The first time, all the way to the twentieth time, we're going to sit Johnny down (time out), have a rational, calm discussion (the short version), along with a consequence that Johnny will *not* like. The consequence should be age appropriate and doable, such as restricted to his bedroom (be certain to remove television and computer privileges or this will just be fun time); or no video games for an hour; or an abhorrent chore that can be completed in a half hour, or removal of a favorite toy for half hour. Remember, two important things: Johnny's brain isn't fully developed yet (we'll discuss this in due time also), so you will have to repeat this discussion/consequence for a very, very long time, each time with calm rationality; and the consequence must be felt. If you simply discuss and then just restrict him to his room for an hour for him to play on his computer or watch television, he isn't going to feel the consequence and therefore isn't likely to stop repeating the negative offense.

Having a bookshelf full of books in a child's room will give them quality educational time if restricted to their bedroom.

One of my favorite consequences when my daughters broke one of my rules was to send them outside to pick up pecans for half hour. Oh, but they hated that task, but I loved it because it cleaned up the yard in preparation for mowing the following spring. Bwahahaha—parental revenge is soooooo sweet.

Still, there needs to be a balance (this is another thing you're going to see me write a lot about in this book). Children cannot face consequences merely for *negative* actions. They also need to know that they will be noticed when they accomplish something *positive*. Still, even though the consequence is a positive one, we need to avoid those extremes. After all, if we give Janice a car for getting straight As in high school, how are we going to top that? A jet when she graduates college with honors?

So, let's add to our parental game plan, how to reward positive behavior. Again, a template will serve for all rewards throughout childhood. You don't need a reward system for every potential action that a child will do in their young lives.

Some experts feel that verbal recognition is sufficient. A tactic referred to as intrinsic rewards. Making a child feel competent and valued for the accomplishment should be satisfactory, and if that's your take, then simply ensure you do so consistently; however, I'm old school, and I believe in extrinsic rewards in combination with intrinsic. Extrinsic rewards are tangible rewards that a child can touch, feel, enjoy in the moment. So, our template for all positive rewards should be verbal recognition along with a simple, affordable tangible reward. Unless you are anti-tangible rewards. If it isn't a major task completed, a simple acknowledgement will suffice.

Let's say that Janice cleans up her room consistently. We should let her know we're pleased with her efforts and perhaps give her a weekly allowance for her to save or spend.

One thing I must mention here. There's a behavior I've witnessed in fellow teachers, which I recommend avoiding at all costs. That behavior is excessive or hollow praises. Here's an example of one witnessed regularly at school:

Teacher: "Are you and Tiffany in charge of collecting recycling today?"

Tiffany: "Yes ma'am."

Teacher: "Excellent! Way to go! You're doing a fantastic job. Keep it up. I'm proud of you both."

The children's reaction was to roll their eyes. Why? Because the teacher's recognition of their *assigned* task that week was ridiculously overboard, disproportionate to the chore. I've seen this occur with parents also:

Parent: "My little darling was an absolute angel this morning. Thank you, Miguel, for being such a wonderfully behaved boy. I appreciate you soooooo much" (scoops into arms for excessive hugs and kisses).

The child's reaction: "Mom, stop!" (Squirming to get free). Why? Because the mother went overboard with her praises, which the boy was embarrassed by.

Children are not morons, despite having a still-developing brain. If you gush praises over every little thing they do, they'll catch on quick and eventually your praises will mean nothing. How could these scenarios have gone differently? By simply acknowledging the child and his or her efforts.

Teacher: "Are you and Tiffany in charge of collecting recycling today?"

Tiffany: "Yes ma'am."

Teacher: "Well, thank you both for your assistance. It's very much appreciated."

NEXT

Parent: Miguel was very helpful this morning. He got ready without fussing. Thank you, Miguel. It helps Mommy a lot when you behave well. Hug and kiss goodbye?"

Children appreciate being spoken to in a manner that makes them feel as if they are behaving "grown up", so try speaking to them in a way that doesn't say they are still babies—or idiots.

Another point I need to interject here is that children will often misbehave as a way of getting their parents' attention. It may be negative attention resulting in an unpleasant consequence, but a child who is either starved for parental attention; or who is so used to getting parental attention constantly and then suddenly doesn't get that attention, will do whatever they think is the most effective method for getting attention. Let's think about that for a minute.

Do you, as a parent, give a lot of attention when a child misbehaves—even if it is in giving a lecture or yelling at them? When they behave, is a passing comment all they hear, or nothing at all? Well, in their little brains, having a long conversation with their parent is preferable to not hearing from their parent at all—even if the result is time out or sent to their room.

Here's something else to think about: When you get on to your child for something, do they begin to pitch a fit? Screaming, crying, or hitting? This is a diversionary tactic. A child's way of avoiding a consequence. Another diversionary tactic is to try to change the subject. I've seen children as young as three engage in diversionary tactics.

As related to pitching a fit, think about your reaction? Do you give your child a lot of attention during that time—even negative attention? *"Stop it! You're behaving badly!" "Do you want me to get angrier than I already am?" "You're driving us crazy. You need to stop!"* Think about it? By reacting and responding to your child's temper tantrum, you are adding fuel to the fire. So then, how do we deal with that attention-seeking? Ignore them.

If they are in trouble, follow the game plan: sit them down on the time out chair, tell them what they did, and supply a consequence. If they start to scream, cry, or hit—walk away with instructions that they will be able to leave the chair as soon as they regain control, and then the consequence given will begin (a chore, restriction to their room, no video games for half hour…whatever you said the consequence would be, you need to ensure it is carried out as soon as the fit pitching ends). Then leave their vicinity.

If the child gets up and attempts to bring their screaming, crying, hitting to you, they are looking for that attention. Keep it brief—take them back to the chair and repeat that they will be able to get down as soon as they regain control. Do not hug, kiss, console, or give any other positive attention. Remember, we are trying to teach them that their behavior is not acceptable, and if we coo and kiss on them when they're behaving poorly, it's reinforcing that poor behavior, so they *will* repeat it. They need to know we're displeased without giving too much attention to the behavior. And remember—this must be done consistently; every single time, until the pattern changes, until the habit is broken.

As for the tactic of attempting to steer the conversation away from them and their behavior, don't allow it. Firmly state that they need to put on their listening ears and look at you, then repeat the infraction, and the consequence, and then implement it immediately.

Now that we've started developing our game plan, let's move on to how to talk to our children without allowing our own emotions to wreak havoc.

Humor vs Sarcasm or Threats

Humor is essential in life. It does so much for us—from keeping us healthy to reducing stress. When caring for children, it's an absolute life saver. All of our children picked up on mine and/or my husband's wit—seriously twisted. We *define* dry wit. We both love to laugh, when being serious isn't required (there's a time and a place for everything).

However, what I had to learn is that our twisted sense of humor needed to be tempered when communicating with our children because they simply didn't get it prior to a certain age. In fact, children up to about age eight, take everything a parent says as fact, so if you jokingly threaten to feed your four-year-old to a bear, they may not find the humor in it.

Yes, my husband did this. I laughed, but our youngest didn't. Her eyes grew round as saucers and we had to quickly explain that "daddy is only joking". Now, at eleven, if daddy says he's going to feed her to some local wildlife, she retorts quickly or just laughs. Some of her banter is her father reincarnate, and it's wonderful to witness.

Today, our children will text when dad and I are on a date and say the most outlandish things: "Hey y'all, just wanted you to know that we're going light on the weed tonight and we'll be careful not to burn the house down during our wild party." To which we'll return text: "Okay, just stay away from the cocaine in the closet, and make certain the house is rebuilt before we get home." Shocking, I know, but we certainly laugh a lot (and no, we don't use drugs in our home, at all).

However, when communicating with our younger grandchildren or the daycare children, our humor is age-appropriate and we're cautious to keep the sarcasm at bay, using it not at all. We speak to the younger children completely different than we do our older children. My husband and I both have come to understand that humor is good, funny sarcasm is too—after a certain age.

What is sarcasm? Sarcasm is a negative way of replying to someone. It will generally elicit laughter because even though cutting, it can be humorous. Still, it's meant to be caustic and used with children can prove detrimental to their self-esteem. Here's a few examples:

Charlie: "Mom, can you help me with my homework. I don't understand it?"

Mom: "Well, we're not the brightest crayon in the box, now are we?"

Do you think this child appreciated his Mom's wit? Not really. He's struggling and needs support.

Sarcasm can generally be tempered with tone. Similar to the tone we'll discuss related to discipline, sarcasm is more biting if the tone is sharper.

Along with doing our best to curb our natural inclination to be sarcastic with children, is the urge to threaten. Even if playfully, younger children simply won't get it. In the south, we have an unwritten rule that, if you don't threaten someone on a regular basis, you don't love them: "Yeah, you just try to get off of that chair and I'll glue your bottom to it." "You back talk me again and I'll pour Super Glue in your mouth" "Either come now, or I'll just leave without you" "Back talk again, and I'll shoot you". Would any of these scenarios occur? No, of course not, but no longer is this mode of speech acceptable, and it needs to be avoided altogether with children under eight. After eight, children are more capable of comprehending the tone and the non-serious intent.

My dad and I banter with threats all the time: "Dad, either you take care of your health, or I'm going to come down there and make you wish you did." "Well, come on then. I can still whoop you." "Oh, I don't think so. I can take you easily." This is generally done with a light loving tone, which tempers the threats. My dad knows I love him, and I know, without reservation, that he loves me.

Just as with discipline. Tone is everything.

So then, the rule of thumb when using humor and/or sarcasm, is to wait until a child is at least eight years old and can more readily comprehend the intent of the message. Under eight, address children in a respectful tone that makes them feel competent and "grown up" but avoid verbiage that cannot be translated by their brain at that age.

How do I get my child to listen to me?

I address this piecemeal beneath quite a few sub-headers, but there is a couple of ways I address my own children. Let's start this section with two phrases that I use constantly. The first, is to ensure that my children are listening to me: "Repeat what I just said"; and the second is to ensure that they remain safe: "Do first, ask why later".

I discuss the "repeat what I just said" in more detail later also, so I'll just touch on it here. Children listen to things that interest them. You telling them that they need to do a chore is not one of those things, so they will not hear you. However, if you issue the instruction and then say, "repeat what I just said", then you are 1) ensuring your instruction is heard, and 2) ensuring they don't have an excuse for not following through. Again, I'll discuss this in further detail shortly.

As related to safety, my children grew up hearing, "Do first, and ask why later". When they first asked me why, I explained, "Because your life may depend on it". *Really?* Yes, really.

If my child runs into the street and there is a car headed his way, all I have time to do is yell: "Get out of the road!" If my child decides to ask me "why" ... or

We're out hiking, and cross paths with a rattler. "Casey, stand absolutely still!" If my child doesn't listen, but decides to ask me "why" and keep walking...?

There were a few times in our lives when I'm glad my children heeded this protocol because their lives *did* depend on it. One of which was the rattlesnake scenario. We were hiking and there was a rattler near the path, its tail rattling a warning as we neared. Imagine if I'd instructed my child to stop moving and they'd ignored me with a "why" and kept on walking? I shudder to think. To instill this into my children for it to become habit, I require it in all areas, not just life-threatening scenarios. After all, life-threatening scenarios don't happen all the time, so it would be difficult to drill this into them if I only had those times to reiterate it. To make it a habit, I require it with every instruction, no matter how benign. For example:

"There's a dog headed our way off leash, walk behind me until we pass". Sometimes my children will want to ask why, and there isn't a reason why I couldn't just answer their query. However, it's a good instructional tool for making the "do first, ask why later" instinctive. So, instead of answering, I repeat, "Do first, ask me why after we've passed the dog." Invariably, they'll ask the moment we pass the dog, and I'll respond, "Because this is not an off-leash park, and that person is breaking the law. Also, even though the dog is friendly, we don't want to encourage law-breaking." (Yep, this occurred and yes, I actually said that. Can you tell I'm not fond of lawbreakers?).

In general, getting a child to listen is directly related to how you speak to him or her. Do they know you're the one in charge? Do you wait until you have their full attention before trying to tell them something? Do you have them repeat what you said? Do you use the proper mode of speech? Are you screeching at them?

Mode of speech, or tone, is another thing I address frequently throughout this book. If we speak to our child in a firm tone that says we're serious and we're the ones in charge, they are more likely to listen to us; if we communicate well and in a manner that doesn't treat them like morons, they are more likely to listen to us. In the end, whether our child listens is directly related to how we're coming across to them. Are we being sarcastic or snapping, or are we speaking in a calm manner? Are we yelling and being hysterical, or have we learned to speak to our children without losing our cool? Let's look at that particular area in more detail.

How to talk to children without blowing your top

Children are manipulative monsters. From the moment they realize that they can cry and elicit a response (you pick them up); to wooing and cooing you into borrowing the car when they just barely learned how to drive—children are master manipulators. Some people think this is a survival mechanism; that children (and a lot of adults) manipulate to survive in a very harsh world. Perhaps they're correct, but it isn't the best survival method and when it fails—and it ultimately will fail—all hell breaks loose.

Still, they are going to try, and many times their efforts are going to drive parents to the brink of insanity, to the abyss of fury. Bear in mind, that parents are already hanging on to sanity and inner peace by a quickly unraveling, very thin thread, so when children start in on their manipulations, when they have a meltdown because they can't find their favorite shoe, when they start bickering because one looked at the other cross-eyed…it's easy to imagine why parents blow their tops.

I talked about Zen in the introduction, and I will reiterate that it may just be a good idea to get used to finding calming techniques as well as formulating positive reinforcement methods, *before* they are needed. The more positive you are, the more likely it will be that your children will be also. It will also assist in saving your saneness.

"Right from the beginning, it's critical that children have experiences and relationships that show them they are valued, capable human beings who bring pleasure to others. Positive attention, reactions and responses from key grown-ups help children build a picture of how valued they are". (4)

Now, am I referring to that type of behavior where anger is completely anathema? Absolutely not. I'm referring to a balance. Children need to know when you are pleased and when you are not pleased; and if you constantly feign a smile or never lose your temper, how will they know you are displeased? And by "lose your temper", I do not mean screaming the house down, punching a hole in a wall, slapping your child, etc. Here are some keys to disciplining without the need for a trip to the shed or the psychiatrist to save your mind. The following two tactics will work with any age: tone and word usage.

#1—Tone. Your tone is key. There is a saying that you can generate more fear with a calm tone than with yelling. *Huh? I don't think so,* you're probably thinking. After all, we've all seen people cower in the face of rage; however, what we've all probably witnessed later is that the rage soon becomes a sort of joke: *Yeah, yell all you want, I know you for the coward you are.* There is also a train of thought that if you lose your temper, you lose control and are affecting your health in the process. I believe that to be factual. In fact, it's backed up by science. Let's take a quick peek at what happens to our bodies when we get overly angry, to the point that we're yelling and screaming, instead of remaining calm and rational.

The amygdala in our brain is what controls our temper, and children are going to ensure that our amygdala gets a huge workout during the eighteen years prior to them moving out of the house. So, let's see what happens to our brains when our children are going ballistic over something you said to them, are backtalking, disobeying, disrespecting, or fighting with each other.

The amygdala is triggered. Soon after, the adrenal glands jump in, releasing adrenaline and testosterone, which makes reasoning with your own brain even more difficult, so forget about reasoning with a child.

If we react instinctively, yelling back or striking out physically; if we don't learn calming techniques and to use *tone* to our advantage, science shows that we're hurting our bodies. "According to a 2009 study in the Journal of the *American*

College of Cardiology, subjects who were angry had a higher risk for developing coronary heart disease. Older studies also point to angry people showing signs of accelerated decline in lung function, speeding up the natural process of aging. Frequent rage is no good for your mental health...; a 2012 study by Concordia University researchers found that anger seemed to hinder treatment and worsen conditions of patients who suffered from anxiety disorders" (5)

Developing calming techniques and using a specific tone, however, can train children early on to distinguish when we're pleased and displeased, allowing our amygdala to take a vacation, and sparing our physical, long-term health. It's a technique, so takes practice. Again, am I saying that we should never get angry? Absolutely not. It's just to our advantage to get angry in a way in which we maintain control; not allow a child to gain control. Let's continue with how to use a proper tone when addressing our children.

Elevated, cheerful tones say, "I'm happy and not upset with you in the least." A stern tone immediately says, "Whoa, you're doing something that goes against my rules or is improper and we're going to need to address this".

Using tone instead of our temper tells that child that we're the one in control and we're not going to allow them to either drive us out of our minds, or to allow them to break our rules. Using a calm, stern tone, also gives children a good example on how to handle disagreeable encounters when they grow up.

#2—Word usage. Sounds like we're in grammar class, but in reality, how you speak to a child makes all the difference in their behavior. Tone isn't the only way in which to get your point across. Using the proper words can make a big difference also.

A. Avoid the word "no" from early on. The word "no" is a monosyllabic word that children pick up on quickly; and said enough times by parents will be one of the more frequent used. It will also become the bane of mom's and dad's existence. Try using harder phrases combined with redirection. Hmm. What does that mean?

Well, here's an example. When your darling baby girl attempts to touch your expensive laptop for the first time, your instinct may be to shout, "No!" and perhaps put out a hand and push them away.

Through this action, your child is learning two negative behaviors: to shout "no" and to push people.

However, let's shift that instinct and put some effort and thought into what we need to do. Try using positive words and redirection. They aren't going to have a clue as to what you're doing, but eventually they will. Let's rework that scenario.

Little Natasha crawls over and reaches for that expensive laptop. In a stern tone, we'll say: "Natasha, this is a *non-touchable* item. Let's see about finding a toy for you to play with."

We're not going to use our happy tone, because we want Natasha to know what she's doing is incorrect behavior. If we use our happy tone, she will turn it into a game. Natasha *isn't* going to process this after one time and will repeat her attempts to touch your computer frequently; however, if you repeat your own actions consistently, it will sink in…eventually. How do I know this is effective? I use it daily in training my daycare children what is permissible to touch and what isn't (*non-touchable item*), and where they are and are not allowed to roam (*boundaries*). I repeat those two phrases/words numerous times a day, but the children who have been with me the longest no longer attempt to leave their boundaries and don't touch things without asking first, or things I've designated as non-touchable.

I have in my care a delightful three-year-old who's been with me since six weeks of age. When he started crawling, I started instruction. Children instinctively want to go wherever they aren't supposed to. I have gates up to help them learn their boundaries, but invariably, they will attempt to go behind them. "Boundaries," I say. They stop and look at me because my tone is firm, and they can sense I mean business. They crawl over and try to touch something I'd prefer they not get in the habit of touching (i.e. my laptop). "Non-touchable item," I say. Again, they stop and look at me because my tone is firm, and they know I mean business. They don't have a clue, at crawling age, what I'm saying, but they do know I'm not cooing at them. Over a period of six months or so, after repeating continually, they start to realize that those two words/phrases mean they aren't doing something permissible, and not long after that, they stop trying to bypass their boundaries or touch my laptop altogether. My three-year-old darling will now ask, "Can I touch this?"

Tone is just as effective for a teenager who asks to spend the night at a friend's house after spending the afternoon breaking every rule in your house (hopefully not).

The wrong tone will tell your teenager that he or she hasn't committed any grievous act against you, so he or she will quickly become confused if you cheerily reply, "Sorry darling, but you'll be staying home tonight."

However, just as confusing would be an uncontrolled outburst. "Are you out of your ever-loving mind? Do you really think you're going to get to go anywhere after acting like a total butt?" Remember balance is key and the right tone is imperative. "For you to be able to go to your friends for the evening, you're going to have to adjust your behavior in our home first. We'll see how it goes next week and discuss a sleepover then." (Later, you're going to get to a section entitled *Prepare to be hated*. This is just a taste as to why). Does this mean that your teenager is just going to accept what you've said? Perhaps they may if they've grown up hearing the proper tone from you. Likely not, however, since they aren't getting what they want and are at that age where making your life a living hell is their primary goal. We'll cover teenagers more in a bit.

The actual word "no" isn't a no-no. After all, children need to be able to answer a question with a "yes" or "no". The way I'm referring to its usage, is strictly when disciplining. Finding an alternate method in which to address a child's behavior over saying "no" will prevent this word from issuing from their two-year-old lips at every chance they get.

B. *Use "naughty" not "bad"*—Children are inherently "good", not "bad", so we want to reinforce that. We can do this easily by avoiding the word "bad" when we discipline them. Even saying, "What you did was bad!" indicates that they themselves are. Instead, address the behavior, "Throwing sticks at the dog is naughty". This goes hand-in-hand with three other methods of speech...

C. Positive, non-accusatory, inclusion wording—Huh? I grouped these three together because they generally work in concert. *Positive wording* is self-explanatory. We want to use words that lift not put down; words that are encouraging, not bashing; words that address the behavior, not attack the person...let's stop there, and talk about that last one. A lot of times, parents will phrase things, unintentionally, to make it sound as if the child is bad and is doing something deliberately naughty. Maybe they are, but we want to avoid pointing that out. Said enough times, a child will begin to believe it, and live it. If, however, we address the behavior and not condemn the child, they will realize it's the behavior that's unacceptable, not them.

Next, try to avoid accusations when addressing a behavior.

Finally, try not to make it all about the child. If you use *inclusion wording*, it makes it sound as if you are all in it together, as a family, and can rectify the behavior as a family. Since these all go hand-in-hand, let's look at a scenario using all three *incorrectly*.

"I told you not to touch that! Why can't you listen when I talk to you? If you had listened to me, you wouldn't have broken my plant! How many times have I told you not to run in the house? Now, I have to pay for another plant. Did you do that on purpose just to get even with me? What you did was very bad!"

Instead of positive, uplifting words, this Mom used negative, accusatory, exclusion words. This child was not a part of the family at that time; she was someone who did something bad and was attacked for it (yes, these were actual words used toward a child).

Let's look at how this scenario could have gone a little smoother; and remember, we're going to use our not-pleased-stern tone.

We have a rule in this house about not running, because when we run, something can get broken. In this instance, that something broken is my plant. In order to replace this, we're going to allow you to contribute your allowance toward a new one. In future, we're going to remember that the no-running rule is in place for a reason. Thank you.

Did she just write "thank you"? Yes, I did. Manners are something we want our children to learn, and if we plan to teach them to say *please* and *thank you*, we must set the proper example. Even when issuing a command, we should preface it with *Please* and conclude it with *Thank you*. I'll address this more later. As for the above scenario…

Instead of singling out the child with "you" and "I"; and attacking with negatives, the words used are "we" and the action is addressed. The consequence for the action is given using positive terminology. Concluding with a positive reminder of the rule broken. Will the child be happy about the reprimand? No. Will the child be thrilled that he or she is going to lose his or her allowance? Not at all. Will he or she attempt to argue with you? Without a doubt. (Again, I'll address arguing with a child a bit later). Still, it will ensure the child understands the rules, and knows there are consequences to breaking those rules.

D. *Repeat, repeat, repeat.* What's this got to do with word usage, you ask? Well, if you are consistent, you are going to be repeating the same words over and over and over again. Why? Because children just won't get it the first time, second time, or the fiftieth time around. So, knowing how to say things in a calm, positive manner should become habit for you and eventually, your child will realize that you aren't going to waiver or alter your course of action, no matter how absurd his or her behavior becomes. As with the example of my three-year-old darling earlier, instructing him—and the other children in my care—requires repeating things hundreds of times, daily. It gets frustrating, but I just take deep breaths continually, count to a hundred continuously, and then watch the fruits of my labor as they blossom into well-behaved, well-mannered toddlers. It's worth it, believe me. Okay, so…repeat, repeat, repeat.

Earlier I mentioned a few times that children's brains aren't developed yet. Children may look like tiny replicas of mom and dad, but they are missing one major element that sets them apart: they don't have a fully developed brain yet, nor will they have until they reach adulthood. That's why repetition is key to development and learning. Over the course of their lifetime, they will slowly require less repetition because things will start to make sense as cognition develops. Two and two start to equal four. Until then, keep your patience in check and learn to say things over and over and over again, reminding yourself that it will sink in—one of these days.

A lot of parents tell me, "I've said that a hundred times. Why can't they remember?" Well, let's take a quick look at how children's brains are different, which will readily explain why we need to calmly repeat, repeat, repeat.

"Neuropsychologists and parenting advisors (at least those who have a knowledge of neuropsychology) often try and calm parents down when they are pulling their hair out over their teens' rude, moody, disorganized, risk-taking, impulsive behaviors. The frontal lobes (or more correctly, the prefrontal lobes) of the teenage brain, they tell the parents, are still developing. By the age of twenty to twenty-five, the frontal lobes will be fully mature, and the impossible teenager will morph into a normal person—a fully functional, socially well-adapted adult. This is not simply psychobabble but backed by numerous brain and social behavior studies". (6)

As infants, babies, and toddlers precede the teen years (obviously), then we know that their brains are even less developed than teenagers, so communicating with them takes just as much patience and even more repetition.

Let's look at the differences. Figure one, below, created by Paul Thomson at the UCLA neuroimaging lab, demonstrates the development of the brain from childhood to adulthood. The prefrontal cortex, the part of the brain not fully developed in young people, is that part that is responsible for logical thought. Moreover, "the frontal lobe is the part of the brain that controls important cognitive skills in humans, such as emotional expression, problem solving, memory, language, judgment, and sexual behavior. It is, in essence, the "control panel" of our personality and our ability to communicate". (7)

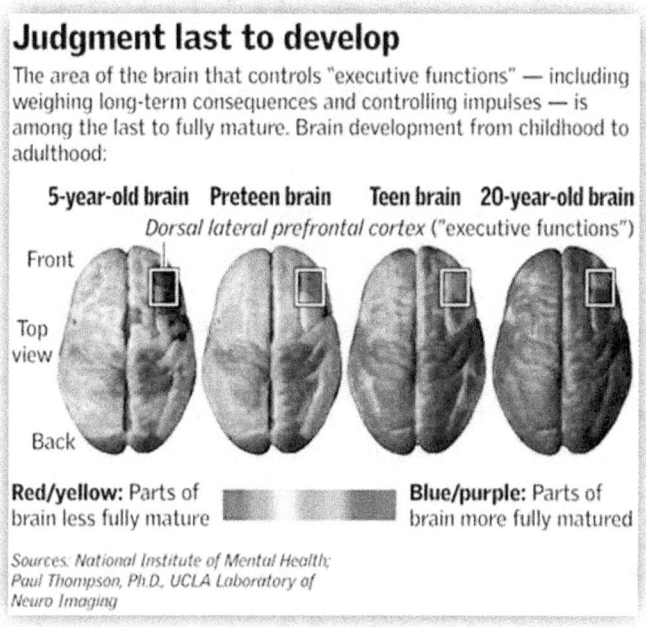

So then, if parents can come to the realization that a child's brain is still under construction, it may just be easier for them to reconcile all the aggravating behaviors that create havoc. Combine this knowledge with a parenting plan, and you may just survive until your children reach adulthood.

The above information related to a child's brain development will hold truth and value from birth to age twenty-one (or longer for some), so it may be repeated a couple of more times before the end of this book. After all, repetition is key to learning, yeah? So then, let's continue with the next item related to disciplining that will ensure we parents maintain our sanity as our children grow up.

Instruct/teach boundaries

Remove the cause. A lot of times we blame the child, when we could have easily resolved the situation by removing the temptation. It's similar, believe it or not, to yelling at a dog for eating off a plate left lying around. Well, had you not left the plate lying on the floor, the dog couldn't have gotten to the food—so whose fault is it? The same holds true for little ones. They are explorers, filled with curiosity over their worlds, and therefore will get into and a hold of anything and everything in their path. So, we can tell them, until we're blue in the face, "don't touch that", "stay away from there", get out of there" or we can make life easier by teaching them boundaries (I used that word earlier). This is a word I use every day with frequency. Still, there are tactics we can employ to assist with use of the word.

Put child locks on cupboards and closets. Place gates around areas that we don't want them to get to (similar to placing gates at the head of stairwells). They *will* attempt to go around those gates, as I mentioned earlier, but putting them there and saying "boundaries", will assist in letting them know we don't want them behind that gate. Redirect when they reach for a non-touchable item. Don't blame them—instruct them.

I have a three-year-old who has been in my care since she was six weeks old. On days when no other child is in attendance, I don't worry over putting up gates, because she's learned her boundaries and knows where she is and isn't allowed to be; what she is and is not allowed to touch. Did that happen in one day—of course not. It took six-to-eight months of constant repetition, beginning at about eight months of age, for it to sink in.

I also have a fifteen-month-old who has also been with me since six weeks of age. When she learned to pull herself up, she immediately set to reaching for my laptop with every intention of popping on the keys much like Mrs. Barbara does when inputting their daily feeding/diaper changing information on the daycare website. She simply wanted to do what Mrs. Barbara was doing. However, it wasn't my intention to allow her to smack on my laptop, so the training on boundaries began: "Sweetheart, this is a non-touchable item. Let's find something else to play with" (stern tone). That instruction began at about ten months of age. Now at fifteen months old, she will crawl over and stand next to me, look as if she wants to touch the laptop, but all I need to say is, "non-touchable". She doesn't touch it. Boundaries being learned.

We can pull our hair out and get frustrated, or we can be parents and instruct. Don't blame the child if all you do is say "No, don't…" without redirecting them or removing the temptation from their reach.

Quick note: I use more phrases than just *boundaries* & *non-touchable*. I also use *behave* and *stay out of mischief*. I also use explanations in addition to certain words until they begin to comprehend the reasoning and then I can just use the one word. Example: "Boundaries, please. Your play area is over here, not behind the gate."

"Because I said so" is a big no-no

When parents get frustrated or are too tired to deal with a child's demands or outbursts, an instinctual response is to shout, "Because I said so…" Problem solved, right? After all, you're the boss in your home, so that should suffice in putting an end to a child's tantrums, nagging, demands, or other negative irritants.

It should also be removed from your repertoire immediately. Avoid this parental pitfall by learning that explanations will serve you better than avoidance—every time. Even though children's brains are not developed fully, remember it doesn't make them morons. They are searching for reason and understanding in every single part of their lives, so give it to them. Even at the youngest age, speaking to your child in a rational manner will assist in developing the habit for when they finally are able to comprehend what you're talking about. However, let's give an example of when they've reached a comprehending stage.

Ten-year-old Rebecca comes to you and asks to purchase an expensive cell phone. She wants one because all her friends have the latest and greatest, so why can't she? Do you really think she's going to comprehend if you say, "Because I said you can't"? Of course not, because her undeveloped mind needs to fill in the gaps between your "No" response and the reasons for that "No" response. If you just say, "No" then, guess what? Her brain is going to fill in the blanks all by itself: "Oh, I can't have a new phone because my parents hate me!" "Oh, I can't have a new phone because they're just too cheap!"

Supply the missing data along with the "No" and the brain is appeased; and, for goodness sakes, don't be vague. That's just as bad as not providing an example at all:

"We're sorry, Rebecca, but you aren't responsible enough."

"Yes, I am. You told me just yesterday that I was behaving very responsibly."

That will start an argument that you don't need. Guess what though—as mentioned, we're going to discuss arguing with a child later as well.

Back to demand and supply. When offering up an explanation for a "No", the best course is always an honest one. If you can't afford that expensive phone, say so. If you're concerned that she'll break it, say so. If you're worried over her losing it or someone stealing it or any other myriad reasons, say so. Don't leave room for doubts, questions, or arguments. Not that your darling child won't argue nonetheless; however, by providing sufficient explanation, it will give them far less ammunition in their arguments.

Don't be pushed to extremes

"I'm going to belt you until you can't sit down". Threats and extreme measures will lead to only one thing—trouble. Parenting extremes generally sprout from aggravation, anger, frustration…those negative emotions we discussed. Well, if you lose your temper to the point where your discipline becomes extreme, you're going to face another of the emotions we mentioned: guilt. And if that doesn't faze you, there's always the law, who will step in and make life a little more interesting than needs be if you can't contain yourself.

There was a time, way long ago, when we could simply take a switch to a child's backside, but those days are long gone. Too many people are watching and are ready, willing, and able to rat you out to the police if you so much as pat your kid on the head with what they perceive as too much force.

Yes, you and I both wish that people would still mind their own business, but since they won't, we must adapt. And, admittedly, there are those parents who go to such extremes regularly, that a call to CPS or the police can only do the child good.

The good news is, if we evolve and use positive training techniques, there will be less reason to pick up that switch or have someone call social services or the police.

Here's an example of extreme parenting that I saw just as I began writing this book. On one of our local news affiliates, a story aired on June 3rd of a man who wanted to teach his son a lesson for being disrespectful. His idea of a proper lesson? To abandon his child in the woods. This was not a teenager, it was a child, less than ten years of age. Not surprisingly, law enforcement had to become involved when the father returned to the site to collect his son and the boy was nowhere to be found.

I'd say that man's life became far more interesting than he intended, and he'll now be under a microscope for some time until all those lovely child protective agencies determine he's a fit dad.

To avoid going to extremes even when your child has no such compunctions: take a step back, draw in several deep breaths, count to twenty, get out of your brain for a minute…or all the above. Your child's meltdown isn't going anywhere, so take all the time you need so that you can address the madness in a calm manner, so that you can discuss the situation without being drawn into an argument, so you aren't tempted to beat your child to within an inch of their life…so you can be the parent.

Now that I've discussed some of the relevant disciplinary actions as it relates to *any* age group, let's break parenting down into *individual* age groups, and discuss all of those lovely, maddening traits that make us wonder why we had them in the first place.

PART 3: Parenting through the ages

"Scientists know that the first five years of life are very important for building a baby's brain. In fact, everything you do and say can help to 'wire' your child's brain - for thinking, feeling, moving and learning. (8)

Newborns

Ah! That bundle of joy has finally arrived, along with the fevers, rashes, crying, sleeplessness, continual feedings, and diaper changes.

While you've worked on and developed that nice game plan for your children, the first six-to-eight months you needn't worry about anything but the above list. Children, in the first six-to-eight months are innocent; incapable of anything more than driving their parents crazy. So, if you've discussed, and agreed upon, who's going to get up during the night to comfort the little one, feed him or her, and change that diaper, then focus on loving that bundle of joy and the calming techniques you've researched and put into practice (I hope).

While a baby this age is innocent of deliberate intent to cause insanity, they will do so. When your baby starts fussing, draw in those deep breaths, drink that chamomile tea, and remember that you had a child because you sincerely desired a small version of you and your spouse that you could nurture.

Calming techniques are especially vital for the woman who gives birth and will undoubtedly undergo postpartum depression for most of that baby's infancy, until her hormones right themselves again. Because of this hormonal imbalance, it is imperative that the spouse be as compassionate as is capable and assist as much as is able.

Something you should keep in mind is that children during the first five-to-eight months have a reason for crying; that they haven't realized the potential of manipulation yet, so don't hold it against them or take it personally. If your child is crying, it's generally for one of the following reasons: hunger, illness, discomfort (i.e. gas or dirty diaper), or difficulty sleeping. Around six months of age, they may start cutting their first tooth, which may also generate a flow of steady tears (Tylenol to the rescue).

It's around five-to-eight months of age, when children start to realize that their tears influence Mom and Dad. Why the large age gap when I just said that infants to about eight months of age are innocent? Because all children develop at different speeds. Some will pick up on things faster than another.

Babies

Again, for the first six-to-eight months, your darling baby is generally incapable of manipulation; however, as stated above, infants develop at different speeds, thus they may begin the manipulation phase as early as six months of age. However, most begin at eight months. I can see you shaking your head in disbelief; however, remember, I've reared quite a few and work with this age group daily, so my experience trumps your disbelief. A baby *will* begin to test you, make no mistake, and if you think they're too young and innocent…?

Here's a good test for determining whether your child has reached that special age of controlling you and your spouse. This test will have to take place *after* all other reasons for those tears have been ruled out: feeding, changing, burping, not quite nap time, Tylenol administered for aching teeth, and no determined illnesses. Yes, I know, it is a long laundry list of tasks to check when a baby cries; but they are certainly important and require lots of affection and attention, so don't overlook even one of them.

After all other reasons for crying have been ruled out, try lying your baby down. If six months or older, lie them on their belly, so if you missed a gas bubble or two, it would assist in removing that discomfort. Now…wait for it!

Does your child begin wailing immediately? Does he or she stop the moment you coo at him or her; or as soon as your arms reach in and pick him or her up?

Let's see if the little darling repeats the pattern. Lie him or her down. Now…wait for it! If the wailing starts again, immediately, and all possible reasons for the crying have been ruled out—your baby has begun that instinctual ritual for survival—manipulation.

Some research indicates that we should pick up babies as soon as they cry; that they are seeking security and our protection and if we allow them to cry, we are feeding their insecurities; that it creates "more anxious, uncooperative and alienated persons who can pass the same or worse traits on to the next generation". (9)

Poppycock (Oops, did I write that aloud?). Well, there may be research that says we should not allow babies to cry, but it is contradicted. Thank goodness!

Later research indicates it's quite all right to allow a child to cry: "Babies allowed to cry themselves to sleep were not more stressed…nor did they have more behavioral problems". (10) Besides the research supporting not pampering or catering to our child's tears, I've seen the effects on both sides of this argument.

Firsthand evidence: My children never suffered any ill effects from being allowed to cry (for no reason other than seeking attention). In fact, quite the opposite. They learned to sleep through the night (after six months of age), learned never to invade my bed; and did not end up spoiled and pampered.

Whereas I've encountered parents, daily, who cannot abide tears and thus will scoop up a child the moment they set them down because the child begins wailing. Once retrieved, the tears miraculously stop. Toting a baby around all day does make accomplishing other tasks difficult, to be certain. If you bring a baby to sleep in your bed for the same reason, you are going to lose even more sleep than when they were first born and needing feeding every two hours of the day and night.

Again, however, remember that this doesn't relate to infants up to approximately six months of age. If those darlings are crying, they have a legitimate reason; also remember: if your child, over six months, is crying, check for all potential reasons for those tears first and rule them out before allowing your child to cry for a short bit.

Still, I do have a specific methodology for when to allow children to cry. I'm not a complete heartless psychopath.

Quite simply, if you've covered all the bases for the tears, and a child begins weeping hysterically the moment you lie him or her down (for naptime or bedtime, or just set them down to play independently)—walk out of the room or go sit down somewhere nearby. If they are still crying after fifteen minutes, return, and do the round of checks again. Diaper clean: *check*, diaper rash: *nope*, sick: *no signs*, burped: *check*, fed: *check*, not too hot/cold: *check*…leave. Do I pick them up? No. Why? Because that's why they're crying to begin with. If I give them what they want, they aren't going to learn. I do the checks and leave. Repeat every fifteen minutes until the little darling discovers that you haven't abandoned him or her; that you are clearly nearby and will come when he or she needs you; and that he or she is not going to get to manipulate you as hoped.

Doing this takes courage and willpower; two traits you'll need to develop if you're going to survive being a parent. I know how much crying tugs at parents' heartstrings; how guilt can overwhelm us into picking them up if we let them cry so much as one minute, let alone fifteen. Still, if we do not allow them their emotional upheavals, they will turn into manipulative monsters; and once that happens, you can go back and correct the mistake; however, altering the behavior once it occurs will be as difficult as climbing Mt. Everest without benefit of climbing gear or oxygen. Think on that before you decide it's heartless to allow your child to cry.

Oh, and this will work with toddlers too. If not implemented at birth, it *will* be more difficult to accomplish and more trying on the nerves, but if you stick with it consistently, the toddler *will* get the message and stop those unnecessary, attention-seeking fussies. Again, however, if you don't want an uphill battle, start in infancy. Now, speaking of toddlers.

Toddlers/Children

Toddlers are so called because they have begun to toddle about. In other words, they are walking; and, as a result, they are more prone to find mischief, which will remain an issue through childhood. Moreover, from toddlerhood through childhood, these darlings will begin, and continue, to test their boundaries, and begin to test your patience with fit pitching, the likes of which you've never encountered before. They will start to exert their opinions over every little aspect of their lives, from what they want to eat to what they want to wear.

The key to surviving this age period, and which will set you up for either success or failure for the remainder of their lifetime, is whether you allow them to be the boss in your home or whether you are ready and able to be the parent that you're supposed to be.

Let me put it this way—you are the owner of a multi-million-dollar corporation. You are in that position because you work hard, have earned the respect of your employees, and won't allow anyone to run roughshod over you. Would you allow an underling to come into your office, pitch a fit, and manipulate you into doing what he or she demands? Of course not! So then, why would you allow a two-year-old to control your home?

Yet, I've encountered parents completely at their wits end by the time their child is two-and-a-half, because they've allowed their child to make decisions early on. No offense to those parents—but turning decision-making over to a child whose frontal lobe—that part of the brain in charge of rational thought, communication, problem solving, and judgement calls—is undeveloped and won't reach maturity until age twenty-one (at least), is completely irrational. There is a reason that parents exist—to train a child how to be an adult. How can a child possibly be trained to be an adult if the child is the one in control of his or her adult-developing education?

So then, how are parents supposed to be the parents when they can barely maintain control of their own minds? Let's get back to our game plan. We've already determined that we're going to discuss certain scenarios with our spouse prior to our child's arrival into the world (scenarios that can actually be discussed for any child's age—it doesn't have to be prior to a baby's arrival into the family), to develop a generalized template for dealing with certain scenarios, so that when mayhem erupts, we won't become so frazzled as to throw up our hands and turn over child-rearing to a child. Here are some of the areas in which toddlers will test their boundaries and parental resolve.

#1—Feeding time. "How can I get Charles to eat what I make him? My answer: "you can't, so accept it". *What? Didn't she just say we're supposed to be the ones in control of our homes?* Yes, I did;

however, trying to force a child to eat something they don't wish to eat will create more hardship than is necessary.

To get around this—some people truly do turn over mealtime to the child: "Well, sweetheart, if you don't want that, can I make you something else?" Yikes! Absolutely not. This parent made two mistakes in one sentence:

1) Used a "permission" term. Beginning sentences with "Can" "Would you" "Do you", etc. are, in essence, giving a child permission to make the decision. We'll discuss this in further detail a bit later.

2) She caved to her child's determination not to eat what she made.

How could she have turned this around? Instead of giving control over to the child, she could set in place a strategy for mealtimes: *time limits.* Toddlers & children will need three primary meals a day and approximately two snacks, set between two-and-a-half to three hours apart. For main meals, give children approximately forty-five minutes to complete their food. Snacks, a half hour.

Well, what then? What if they don't eat? Then they don't eat. *What!? You expect me to starve my child?* Seriously? Do you really think they're going to starve before deciding that food is good, and they don't want to miss out on the opportunity to eat? Remember, children's brains aren't developed yet, but that doesn't make them morons. Also—and this is important—once you've set the time limit, stick to it. Remember—consistency. If you tell your child they have forty-five minutes to eat, and then they declare at the end of that time they aren't finished but have spent the entire time playing about—take their plate and tell them they'll have another opportunity to eat at the next meal. Timers are good for this. They aren't old enough to determine the passage of time, but they can be taught what a buzzer means.

This will train them to use their time wisely and properly; that when it's mealtime, play time is put aside, and that you are the one in charge.

Also, make certain to wait until the next mealtime to provide them food to eat. They will definitely be hungry by then and are less likely to fuss about eating whatever you give them. If you give them food half hour after them rejecting what you made them the first time, because they are whining and crying that they are hungry, then you're teaching them that all they need to do is pitch a big enough fit and they'll get what they want. Wait until the next mealtime and you're teaching them the importance of eating when it's mealtime. Do they have to eat everything presented to them? No. After all, we're the ones dictating the serving size, which may not correlate to their needs at that time.

To ensure that they'll be more inclined to eat what we make them, don't be afraid to make food inviting—add a little cheese or Ranch dressing to that broccoli, or make a game out of it: "The first one to try this new food will get an extra quarter in their piggy bank this week". I prefer not to encourage a competition over who will "eat all of their food first". After all, as stated, we aren't as concerned about them clearing their plates, as we are in getting them to eat at least something. With that being said…

Another thing that might make mealtime a little easier to bear for parents is an understanding that children will eat more, or less, depending upon if they are going through a growth spurt. If they've decided that everything you put in front of them suddenly tastes like dirt and they aren't going to eat it, consider their bodies aren't in need of as much sustenance as when they are going through a growth spurt and will consume anything—including dirt.

There was a time when getting my children to eat what I made was a challenge, so I decided to make things a bit more interesting. To entice my children into eating properly, I decided to change things up a bit. I labeled foods according to their health benefit: "Okay, sweetheart. Drink your *calcium*." "This is milk, Mom." "Yes, but it's also calcium, and what is calcium good for?" (Until they know, I tell them "strong bones and teeth"). "Okay, sweetheart, let's finish that protein. We want to develop strong muscles!" Doing this let's children view their food in a different, positive manner.

Another area that can make feeding a toddler tricky, especially one who is just only beginning to consume adult fare, is when they spit it out. Remember your breathing techniques when this occurs because it is going to be extremely frustrating. You want them to eat; to try new foods; to ensure they get their proper nutrition to grow up big and strong—and they just want to spit it out and make funny faces.

There are methods in which to get a child to eat, but the biggest is to maintain your own patience. If you get frustrated and start snapping, all you're going to accomplish is to upset your toddler and ruin your own day. If you smile, coo, play airplane, eat a little with them…they may still spit it out; however, stick with it. They simply are not familiar with the strange textures and tastes. Once the familiarity sinks in, they will start to eat the food provided.

I mention this because this happened recently in my daycare facility. Our darling fifteen-month-old wasn't certain that she liked spaghetti, causing my daughter no end of frustration, who'd asked to feed her that day. She did her utmost to stay calm, and I'll give her credit for that, but after the child spit out the food continually, she threw up her hands and said, "Mom, she just doesn't like it!" I took over. I cooed and smiled and kept at it. Within twenty minutes, she'd cleared the bowl. My daughter looked at me, "How do you do that?" I just laughed and gave her a hug, "You'll get it too, eventually. The key is patience and perseverance"—and it really is.

#2—Decision making. I've heard parents phrase speech in a manner that leaves the decision up to their children, as young as two. This is what I call "permission phrases". I mentioned this briefly before.

Phrases beginning with "Can we...?" "Would you like...?" "Do you...?" may seem polite verbiage, but in reality, it sets up a child to make decisions they simply are not capable of making. Even something as innocuous as "would you like to wear this today?" sets up the parent for a fight.

Many times, I've seen parents on the verge of a nervous breakdown because they used permissive phrases: "Cynthia went berserk because I *asked* her what she wanted to wear, but she wanted to wear her swimsuit, and when I disagreed, she pitched a huge fit."

Of course, she did because the mom left the decision up to a two-and-a-half-year-old, and when that decision was questioned, the toddler didn't like it. Would you like it if you were given an option and then told your option wasn't a good one?

Remember, children's brains are incapable of problem-solving and decision-making until their frontal lobes are finally developed; so, at this age, especially, they need assistance with how to make appropriate decisions. Obviously, we aren't going to allow them to wear shorts in the winter, but given the chance, they may select that attire because it's their favorite: proof that they are not truly capable of rational decisions early on, even though occasionally they may mimic a rational adult.

Instead of leaving the decision up to them, you must make certain that they know who the decision-maker is, which also provides a positive example of correct decision-making skills. Instead of starting a sentence, "Can we…?" "Would you like…?" or "Do you…?" let's alter it a little. We're still using our manners, but we're not leaving room for argument. We can even provide a reason, so that it isn't just a direct order, rather a logical choice: "Please put on your tennis shoes. Thank you." "Please wear your purple jumpsuit today. It's chilly out. Thank you." "Please ensure you eat your breakfast. You'll need that energy to play. Thank you."

Remember, if you want your child to learn proper manners and speech, it's imperative that you emulate that proper manner and speech. Children are tiny replicas of you, so if you want them to grow up using manners, you must use manners, even when issuing a command.

#3—Temper Tantrums. Temper tantrums are generally the result of:

A. Frustration at being misunderstood. As a child learns communication skills, it can be aggravating when they are unable to vocalize a need or put words to their anger, upset, or other emotions. Instead of losing your own temper, try assisting. Do *not* put words in their mouths or assume you know why they're having a fit. That will just make things worse. Try instead to transfer your calming techniques: "Take a deep breath and think about what it is you're trying to say", or "I'm willing to listen, but we're going to have to calm down to talk. We can't yell, kick, or hit to get our point across."

B. As stated above, taking a decision from the hands of a child who should not have been given that decision to begin with can also cause frustration, leading to a temper tantrum.

C. Sometimes a tantrum is strictly manipulative—whether intentional or not. A child denied what they want may pitch a holy-bloody fit in the hopes of changing their parents mind. This will become habit, especially if it works.

Have you ever been in the grocery store and seen a child start screaming or crying—generally because he or she was denied that box of cereal or candy bar? I have. Many, many times. Think back on some parents' reactions. "Shh, stop fussing. I'll get you an ice cream when we leave. I promise. Just stop embarrassing me" or "Okay, okay, here. You can have it".

Uh oh—that parent has just set themselves up for repeated tantrums because mom or dad were too embarrassed to be the parent; and that child has learned that if they want something, they need only scream the store down and they'll get it.

However, if that parent were to tell that child, "We are in public which means behaving well. If we cannot behave well, not only will that treat not happen, but there will be consequences—especially if I have to postpone my shopping and head home now." Okay, using those exact words are not necessary, but addressing the behavior and the consequences are. It's no different than the game plan for discipline at home, minus the time out.

Will this automatically stop the whining and the tears? Nope. But, repeated consistently, with consistent consequences, will train your child the expectations for when you're in public.

In addition to being aggravating, temper tantrums can lead to physical violence. Here's an example:

A friend of mine regaled me with an incident with her five-year-old, "Today was a disaster from the moment we got up. Jessica didn't want to brush her teeth this morning, and then she wanted to wear her sandals, and when I told her to put on her tennis shoes, she pitched a fit and started hitting Mommy. I admit I lost my temper and popped her on the head. Then we had to have a talk about why we can't hit Mommy."

This was an actual occurrence. The only thing that Mom did correct in that scenario was to discuss why it is not good to hit Mommy. Following the mentality of the day in which adults seem to think giving the child leeway to make their own decisions, this parent told me that she *asked* Jessica which shoes she wanted to wear, and whether she *could* brush her teeth. Well, she *wanted* to wear her sandals (despite being twenty degrees outside and rainy); and that particular morning she *couldn't* brush her teeth, so didn't want to. When forced to do the opposite of the decision she'd made, her little mind snapped; and then her mom snapped.

What could have potentially prevented this temper tantrum? As with boundary training, remove the temptation, or in this instance, remove the underlying cause—allowing the child to make decisions. "Jessica, please go brush your teeth. We need to leave soon. Thank you." "Jessica, here's your tennis shoes. Let's get them on, please. We're leaving in a minute. Thank you."

The reason I said "potentially prevented" is because no matter what methods you employ, your child may invariably decide to pitch a fit, nonetheless. If your child does decide to go ahead and pitch a fit, just reiterate your instructions in a firm tone, or you may give that explanation: "I need you to wear your tennis shoes because sandals aren't appropriate for today." "I need your teeth brushed, because we brush out teeth every morning to prevent our teeth from getting sick, and because we don't want our breath to stink." What you want to avoid, at all costs, is bargaining or negotiating. Your child may seem capable of adult reasoning, but remember, that is just perception due to their ability to mimic us. They aren't capable of rational thought or reasoning. So, if you've given the instruction and they still want to argue, cry, or pitch a fit, or bargain, don't use phrases such as: "Maybe you can wear your sandals tomorrow…" Why can't you say things like this? Because on that tomorrow your child is going to say, "You said I could." "No, I said, 'maybe'" …or… "You said I could." "I know, but the weather isn't cooperating." Either way, you may end up not being able to stick to a bargain, so avoid doing so.

As children get older, temper tantrums may result from being told to do something they don't wish to do; or because that dictate interfered with something they were already doing. Some parents, faced with a child's meltdown may cave and say, "Hey, okay, okay. I'll take care of it", which, of course, gives the child an excellent reason to repeat the tantrum. After all, it got him or her a positive result. For the parent, it may just seem easier to do it oneself than to face the tantrum, but it isn't the best strategy.

Other times, they just aren't ready for what it is you're requesting, and their brain doesn't compute well enough to formulate a rational response. Example: Jimmy is right in the middle of a video game when his mom declares, "Jimmy, go clean up your room please. Thank you."

You'd think, using the proper technique that Jimmy would peacefully acquiesce. Instead, he starts kicking and screaming? Why? Because his mom chose that moment, when he was just about to defeat the Jabberwocky to declare his room was dirty and needed tidying. So, let's re-evaluate and add to our list of how to deter tantrums: timing (we'll also discuss, a bit later, *choosing your battles*).

If his mother set a specific amount of time for game play, then she could easily work around that game play and dedicate time for chores and outdoor time, etc. So, to avoid a meltdown, let's determine to schedule game play, outdoor play, and clean up at separate times of the day. Yes, appointments and other life events are going to interfere with any schedule you create, so learn to be flexible. If you schedule game time for four p.m., but Alexander has a dental appointment at four p.m., shift his game play to another hour of that day; or allow him to play on a hand-held device en route.

For all of you luddites out there reading this who think I'm promoting over-use of technology, cool your jets. It was merely an example of *timing*. Another example I could give: If Jessica is in the middle of reading an engaging chapter, or struggling over a particularly difficult violin piece, you aren't going to interrupt her with a request to clean her room or you can likely expect that tantrum to occur. Time your requests and you're less likely to face opposition.

Still, not many children are going to want to do a disagreeable task and may pitch a fit even if they were doing no more than lying on their bed counting the specks of paint on their ceiling. I've faced those moments also, to which I generally reply, "You can pitch a fit if you want, as long as you do what I requested. Thank you." My reasoning in allowing it? Think about how often you moan and complain about your work, but you still do it…well, I simply translate to the children. Of course, they aren't happy about doing something they don't consider entertaining, so I will give them leave to complain about it…as long as they do it.

#4—*Cling and Cry & Fussing*

This particular section is for the children who cling to their mom or dad, crying to beat the band (an idiom that means they are attempting to out wail a rock band). They are behaving as if they are on a sinking ship, scared half out of their minds, and their parents are their life preserver. Yet, nothing untoward has occurred in which to cause such a reaction—or has there?

Let's explore this further.

There is generally an underlying cause for the start of tears, but when it comes to the "cling and cry" there is a primary outcome that the child is in search of: they want mommy or daddy's attention or do not want mommy or daddy to leave them behind.

So, while we want our child to understand that tears are okay, we need them to realize that hysterics for the sake of attention or without a truly justifiable reason is not okay. Let's explore some of the reasons for the "cling and cry".

Let's say that a child gets in trouble for something. The parent snaps at them. No child likes to get in trouble, so they immediately let lose the tears, to elicit empathy. You're probably thinking at this point: *I don't think a two-year-old is crying on purpose. They just got scared by my tone of voice.* Yes, they did, and they also know how to milk your guilt over causing the tears for all it's worth. I've seen it happen a thousand times. A parent will snap, the child will cry; but…

How does crying turn into the "cling and cry" in this instance? Instead of allowing the tears to run their course, which would likely last only a minute or two (they generally stop as soon as another distraction occurs), the parent suffers a bout of guilt and swoops the toddler up into an embrace, cooing and lavishing loves in an attempt to get the tears to stop (yes, I've witnessed this). To keep the loves and attention coming, the child's tears turn to hysterics—and it won't stop immediately because they now have the full *attention* of the parent.

I've seen this happen a lot; and I've also witnessed how it can be avoided firsthand in my daycare. No matter the age, a child in my care can get in trouble. And no matter how I address the child—using the proper stern tone with my manners—it will result in tears (from some; however, those who've been with me the longest comprehend they did something unacceptable and just say, "Yes, Mrs. Barbara"). Anyway, a toddler will do something unacceptable. I'll say, "Please make certain we don't throw that toy. Someone may get hurt. Thank you" (notice that I don't use permissive speech). Because my tone says they are doing something they shouldn't be, the tears will start up. This is primarily true for one particular toddler who uses this tactic on her parent regularly, and he will immediately scoop her up and say something like, "I'm sorry, sweetheart. You just need to listen to daddy…"

Now, if I did as some parents do and scoop them up and start cooing, "It's alright, sweetheart. You aren't in trouble. We just need to make sure we don't throw things because we don't want to hurt our friends"—well, I'd end up setting a precedence that tells the child it's okay to start wailing louder, because they now have my full attention, and a positive result from their negative reaction.

Instead, I tell them, "You're fine. Now go play. And remember we don't throw toys". The crying may continue for another minute or two, but as soon as they find something else to capture their attention, it will stop as fast as it started. This has been proven time and time again. Ignore the wailing, and it will stop. If you've already set a precedent, it will take some time to reverse the behavior. Habits aren't easy to break once formed. Any habit formed will take ten times as long to reverse; however, it can be done—with consistent patience.

Another scenario which can result in a "cling-and-cry", I discuss beneath the section on *injuries*, relates to when a child falls down and gets hurt (minor boo-boo). The parent's reaction is to get hysterical because "their baby fell down". The parent's hysteria takes an otherwise benign occurrence and elevates it to a drama of mega proportions. The child, who may not have even been that hurt to begin with, will begin clinging and crying because 1) it's a reaction to his parent's mania and/or 2) it's getting him attention.

Side note: Parents need to realize that children will react in direct proportion to the parental behaviors. If a parent is calm, a child will be calm; if a parent is hysterical, a child will likely become hysterical. If a parent is feeling guilty, a child is going to take advantage…big time.

Now let's continue. Another scenario which can create the "cling-and-cry" takes time to develop and will happen as a result of getting a positive outcome the first time around—dropping off a child at daycare, or other venue (i.e. karate practice). Some children do not want to be left with a stranger the first time and will cling and cry in the hopes that their parent will take them home instead. *If* that parent encourages this, it will become habit. Here's an example that happened with a drop-in at my daycare facility:

A single dad needed care for his two sons for one week. When he arrived, he walked the children all the way into the play area and sat with them for twenty minutes. He then made a big production out of leaving, "Now, I promise I'll be back this afternoon to pick you boys up. You have a wonderful day, and make sure you listen to what Mrs. Barbara tells you to do. I love you both. Be good."

Before he could walk away, after that long speech, the boys had time to process his words, and translated them: *he's leaving us with a stranger!* Both boys started crying and clinging to his legs. His response? To sit down on the floor and hug them both, giving them loads of assurances that he wasn't leaving them forever. He then spent another fifteen minutes playing with them.

Well, what do you think happened when he tried to repeat the process; to leave? They went into "cling and cry" mode again. Why? Because it got them a positive response: Dad didn't leave, and he stayed and played with us.

Even a simple acknowledgement of your child's breakdown at being left will result in a repeat performance. I've seen it happen time and again. A parent drops off his child, the child begins to cry hysterically. The parent—either feeling guilty about leaving the child or loving the fact that his child doesn't want to be out of his company—will turn at the door and begin offering encouragement that he'll be back soon.

This generally creates frustration for the parent down the road, especially when he's running late and does not have time for the drama.

I've often told parents, "I can only assure you that your child is safe, and they will cease the tears the moment that you shut the door behind you. I give you my word"—and I've yet to be proven wrong. Why? Because the minute a child gets distracted with play, they forget the reason for the hysteria. I've even taken pictures, immediately after the parent departs, and texted them to the parent to verify that their child is just fine. Don't be afraid to request a picture text from your own provider if you need assurances.

How do we prevent the cling and cry? First, we, as the parent, must learn to contain feelings of guilt over reprimanding our children, or snapping at them, or "abandoning" them at daycare or other venue. Even if we lose our cool and snap, that doesn't mean that the child didn't deserve the reprimand and thus if we apologize for anything, it should simply be for losing our cool. I've done this quite a few times. Despite the advice I give for all the methods a parent can take to remain calm, cool, and collected, I've lost mine on occasion (not often, but a few times), with my own children (I've yet to lose my cool with one of my daycare children. Perhaps because I'm older and wiser now). Anyway, once I've collected my wits, I'll tell my children, "I'm sorry for snapping. I'll try to contain my outbursts." Do I tell them it's okay that they got into trouble? No. Do I make a big deal out of it by feeling guilty and drawing out the apologies with hugs and kisses? No. I simply admit my mistake, quickly and calmly, and then move on.

Now, there is something that I need to address here related to hysterics; and that is: your child may have a valid reason to cling and cry. Sadly, in today's society, children are not always safe and secure as they should be. There are people who will hurt an innocent child without second thought. It's reprehensible, but it does occur. So—if your child refuses to calm when left at daycare, with a relative, when dropped off at karate class, etc., despite employing every possible tactic to cease the "cling and cry" spectacle—take the time to investigate why that may be. How can you do this?

1) Step out of site but remain within earshot. Listen carefully to both your child and to how the person with whom you left your child is responding to the hysterics. Do they offer you assurances, but when you press your ear to the door, are they yelling or rebuking in a negative way?

2) As stated above, ask for a picture to be texted to you within five minutes of your departure. Everyone carries a cell phone nowadays, so this should be easily doable. I do it for my parents without them even asking. Does the picture show your child smiling and engaged in an activity? Or does his face show fear or continued tears? I mean it when I say that most children will cease crying *as soon as* they are distracted by something else (within a couple of minutes). If they are still pitching a fit after five minutes…? If you haven't received that requested picture after five minutes, send a text asking for that picture or an explanation. If they don't send one, turn around and head back to daycare. That warrants investigating, in my opinion.

3) In addition, don't be afraid to ask questions about disciplinary policies at venues where you don't remain in attendance with your child. Mine—for my daycare—are in writing; and are followed. When asked, can the on-site staff produce a written policy? Does the staff sound confident in what they're telling you, or does it sound off-the-cuff (made up)? If asked again, will the responses be consistent? Do you get different responses from different people? These are red flags and should not be ignored.

In conclusion, there are myriad reasons why children will break down into a "cling and cry" imp. However, there are ways to break the habit. Remaining calm, not caving to the impulse to overly comfort, allowing them their tears, ignoring their excesses…all of it takes practice, but can be accomplished. Make it a habit and your nerves will thank you for it. Not only that, but your children will also be less likely to grow up a difficult, unruly, unmanageable, manipulative monster. I had one parent reference her three-year-old as "feral" because of how unruly and disruptive she was at home. Amazingly, that same child was calm and well-behaved when with me. Different parenting styles will result in differing behaviors. That's another reason I state to have a game plan with your spouse and for you both to be on the same page, because if you and your spouse attempt to discipline differently, your child will become confused.

#5—Children are sponges and parrots. Even if you've not had children yet, you've probably heard this at one point or another, and it's absolutely factual. Children's little brains are sponges, and their mouths parrot everything. Which is why we, as the adults, should be cautious about every single thing we do and say, which is why we, as the adults, should model positive, responsible, rational decision-making and behavior. Not the easiest thing to do when we work hard and are stressed over finances, our spouse, or other outside influences. Still, we should be cognizant of our own behaviors and speech, because, by the time your little darling becomes a toddler and then onto childhood, they are becoming miniature replicas of the people with whom they spend the most time.

I often hear children spout things that will generate laughter from adults because it is not something we expect to hear from a child. Oftentimes the something spouted will be far from humorous, causing embarrassment for the parents. Ever hear a two-year-old curse, or say something sexual in nature? Do you really think they know what they're saying? Of course not. They are mimicking someone else. Had the parents, or another person with whom the child spends considerable time, not been the ones to say it first, the child would not have repeated it. And if we laugh or draw undue attention, what do you think is going to happen? That's right—the child is going to repeat it because it brought about a positive, or attention-receiving response.

One time, I was visiting someone with a young child. When the mom asked her son to do something, he responded, "I'll do it when I'm damn good and ready". That child was four years old. He had no idea what he was saying. He probably picked it up from a relative who declared that when asked to do something. Parroting can be cute, but it can also be embarrassing. That old adage, "Think before you speak" is true when around a young child. Young children will not think before they speak, they will simply mimic, so it's important to give them something proper to mimic.

At one time, two of my daughters assisted me in daycare when not in school and I told them this repeatedly: "You are the example for these children, so you must be aware of everything you say and do; everything you say and do needs to provide a positive example." It's hard work, constantly monitoring every word and action around little ones; but then who ever said being a parent was easy? It's the hardest job you'll ever undertake.

There's a country song that many of you may be familiar with entitled *Watching You* by Rodney Atkins (2006). If you're unfamiliar, the lyrics go like this:

Driving through town just my boy and me,

    with a Happy Meal in his booster seat.

Knowing that he couldn't have the toy 'til his nuggets were gone.

A green traffic light turned straight to red.

I hit my brakes and mumbled under my breath,

His fries went a flying and his orange drink covered his lap.

Well, then my four-year-old said a four letter word

    that started with "s" and I was concerned,

so I said "son now where did you learn to talk like that"

He said, "I've been watching you, Dad, ain't that cool.

I'm your Buckaroo, I wanna be like you…"

We are responsible for how our children behave, and if we model positive speech and behavior, that's what they will learn.

#6—Back talking. "How do I stop Carlos from sassing me?" Well, ask yourself these questions: Do you have a sassy mouth? Do you snap frequently when speaking to your children, your spouse, or someone else? Is sarcasm a part of your speech? Well, if your child is back talking already, they

are simply parroting you or your spouse, or someone else with whom they spend most of their day.

Remember, they are tiny replicas of us, so if we want them to change, we must change. We must consider child-raising as a job, and if we do it well and if we do it right, they will turn into responsible, productive, well-spoken adults. If we are concerned about their back-talking, we can assist the change by calmly explaining that we need to speak with a respectful tone. Of course, parents will need to emulate that tone for it to take effect.

I could provide an example of a sassy-mouthed parent and mimicry in reply, but something tells me that there isn't a person reading this who hasn't already encountered this type of behavior—either in their own lives or watching a show or movie. It's rampant in our society, but that doesn't make it right.

#7—*Aggression.*

Here, I get to repeat two things I've already stated—all children will go through one of/or all of three phases: hair pulling, biting, or hitting. These may be physical reactions to something completely innocent. Hair pulling may simply be a by-product of patting on the head (I've seen this happen—a fifteen-month-old mimicking hair-tussling. Fingers get caught, and voila—hair pulling). Biting may be because of teething. Okay, don't laugh—this is feasible. If a toddler is used to carrying a teething ring and doesn't happen to have one, they may substitute another soft, pliable substance—skin. I've seen children reach for an arm and bite down or gnaw, quite innocently. Of course, I've also seen a child bite out of agitation when it was close to feeding time, or out anger over another child reaching for his toy. It can also stem from frustration. My daughter told me that my little grandbaby will bite her older brother when they're playing, if she gets frustrated enough.

Hitting generally comes about because of a parent, an older sibling, or another child hitting. So too, may hair pulling and biting. Mimicry is a toddler/young child's way of learning behaviors.

How do we stop these negative behaviors? First, we must be certain that the child understands that these behaviors are not acceptable using our stern tone. I use the phrase, "that's illegal", and it is. If it were an adult hitting, biting, or pulling hair, they could face charges for assault. Also, saying "that's illegal" keeps me from saying, "No!"

Next, we redirect, finding something for them to play with; or we check the clock to see if it's mealtime. The biting, hair pulling, or hitting may also be the result of bickering over a single toy. By showing them there is more to play with, we nip it in the bud.

If the offense is the result of a child invading another's space, then we simply teach them that space is important. I use the word "space" a lot when working with toddlers. If they are young and I know they can't quite comprehend what I mean, I say "space" and then pick them up and move them, demonstrating what I mean.

Finally, we take a step back and re-evaluate our own behavior? Are we providing a positive role-model for that child? Are visiting relatives in the habit of aggression? Does the toddler have older siblings that pick on each other, or the toddler?

I have a child in care whose behavior will sometimes be startling. This young one smiles often and readily, laughs just as much, and is full of mischief (which I continually focus into positive activities); however, occasionally, he will come to daycare and shove or bite another child. His parents were at a loss as to why the shift in behavior, until they discovered his two older siblings weren't always as nice to this toddler as they thought. Behind closed doors, they would snatch toys away with a "mine", which the toddler would mimic at daycare; or push and hit him. He translated this into negative behaviors at daycare by hitting and biting. He was also watching shows at home with those siblings that were not age appropriate. Once his parents addressed these behaviors in the older children, and changed his viewing habits, his own behavior returned to the smiling, laughing mischief maker he was prior.

Another place that children can pick up less-than-positive behavior is at their daycare (or school). Is the daycare your child going to providing positive role-modeling, redirecting, and using positive disciplinary methods? We do at Laughter and Love Daycare. Either way, it's okay to ask.

#8—*Playtime*. Why am I addressing playtime within a section on "issues"? Because there are certain *adult* behaviors that I've encountered of late that seem to be sweeping the nation as acceptable, providing toddlers and children with a negative representation of life. If you hadn't guessed, I disagree with these particular behaviors. To preface each behavior, I'll provide true scenarios: one which occurred with me and the other, one of my daycare parents, who called seeking council because she was so distraught over what happened to her daughter, then three years old; and the last which happened recently to my daughter and her friend at the park.

Scenario #1—Three-year-old Tabitha, and her mother, were staying with a friend for a while. Tabitha was quietly playing with one of her favorite toys that she'd brought along. Three-year-old Caleb decided it was something he wanted and continued to invade Tabitha's space in an attempt to "share" the toy. When Tabitha refused to relinquish her toy, Caleb ran off and tattled to his mom, who then reprimanded Tabitha's mom for not teaching her daughter to *share*. Tabitha's mom called me: "I was so humiliated, Barbara. What can I do? Caleb is a sweet boy, but he has a habit of breaking things, and I don't think that Tabitha should give away her favorite toy if she doesn't want to."

No, she shouldn't. In my daycare facility, children are taught to share; however, there is an exception to that rule. If the toy is one that cannot be played with by more than one child, it isn't required that it be shared. How can you share a single baby doll? If both children are able to engage in imaginative play with that one doll, so be it. In my experience, however, a single toy meant to be played with by a single child, will result in tattling, hitting, biting, or hair-pulling if not shared.

So, my rule of thumb is—if a toy can be played with by more than one child, it can be shared (i.e., an activities center table or blocks); if not, then it doesn't need to be. This is what my children are taught. If a child seeks to remove a toy from a child playing with it, he or she is redirected to another toy with reassurances that they'll have a turn later. If that toy belongs to the individual playing with it, they do *not* have to share it. Why should they risk someone else breaking their belongings? They shouldn't have to. It's also why I encourage parents to leave their personal toys at home.

What advice did I give the parent? I told her to go and speak to Caleb's mom. Explain that Tabitha's toy is special to her, a toy meant to be played with by one person; that if Caleb wanted to play with Tabitha, they could find something else to play with, when Tabitha was ready.

Too often today, I see and hear children demand that another child give up a toy; to "share" it, because parents are teaching them that "sharing" means one child giving up what they're playing with in order to make another child happy. Forget that the child who has to give up the toy won't be happy. This message is wrong on so many levels! All we're teaching our children is to be selfish; that if we want something, all we need do is demand we get it, and it should be given. This message is flawed and should not be continued. I address this further in the section on *Some additional questions I've been asked* because I was asked quite a lot related to specific incidences.

Another message parents are teaching their child is that negative behaviors should be rewarded. *Seriously?* Yeah, I'm in shock too.

There was an episode of a popular children's television show that we were watching during snack time one day (we no longer watch the show). The show was on sharing. *Excellent*, or so I thought. Here was the basic premise and the underlying message being taught to the children:

Little Red Riding Hood's basket of goodies was stolen by the Big Bad Wolf. When located at the end of the show, Little Red Riding Hood opted to give the Big Bad Wolf her *entire* basket of goodies. Prior to that ending, I thought perhaps that the Big Bad Wolf would be reprimanded for stealing and then perhaps Little Red Riding Hood would offer a token from her basket. Nope—she turned over her entire basket to a thief.

So, basically, we're teaching our children that it's okay to reward negative behavior; and that despite our own personal desire to keep what belongs to us, we must give it all away.

Well, aren't we supposed to teach our children the spirit of giving; that we should teach them to willingly give their worldly goods away?

It comes back down to balance. If a person works hard for what they have; if a child receives a special gift for their birthday—then they should have the right to keep it if they so choose. That doesn't make them wrong or selfish. And we certainly should not be teaching our children to reward negative behaviors with positive rewards, as in the above scenario in which the wolf was a thief yet was rewarded for his negative behavior by being given that which he stole. Remember, we should be teaching our children that there are consequences to all actions—positive and negative; yet this show—and many others I've seen—are attempting to teach our children that a child can do something negative and still have a positive consequence. Shows that promote this message are no longer viewed by children while in my care.

Scenario #2—My neighbor came to my door one Saturday afternoon, "Your daughters are being mean to my daughter." *Oh my*, I thought, *I certainly want to address this, since being mean isn't something I've taught my children.* In fact, I have a saying in my house: "always take care of those smaller than you." My daughters, at that time, were about eight and six. The neighbor's daughter was five. Younger than my two.

"What's happened?" I asked.

"Your two daughters need to play with my Olivia. Oliva said they're being mean."

I had to shake my head and process precisely what he'd said. First, if they were being mean, why would she even want to play with them, but that's what she'd told her dad. I certainly didn't want to misunderstand, so I asked him to explain. He did—

"If Olivia wants to play with your daughters, they should play with her. Instead, they run off to play with other children."

"Is there not a way that Olivia could also go to play with these other children?" I inquired.

"No, she's not allowed to leave our yard."

"I see," I replied thoughtfully. "Well, I do apologize if Olivia's feelings were hurt because my daughter's decided they were ready to go play elsewhere…"

"If Olivia wants to play with your daughters, they should play with her," he interrupted, adamant that my daughters had somehow wronged his daughter.

I'd heard enough and replied, in no uncertain terms, "Sir, if my daughters choose to relocate from your yard to play with other children, I most certainly am not going to tell them they can't do that; and I certainly am not going to demand that they be required to play with your daughter only. That's just absurd."

"I see, well then your daughters are no longer permitted to play with Olivia."

Genuine conversation that I couldn't help but shake my head at as I revisited it here, in this text. At the time, I was taken aback. Still, I recall thinking, *well, that solved that, didn't it?* After all, he'd just declared that my daughters would no longer be allowed to play with his daughter. But that wasn't the end of it. Not quite, anyway. A few weeks later, the same man showed up at my doorstep with an invitation to Olivia's birthday party.

"I expect they'll come," he said.

"No, they won't be there. We have a prior engagement which conflicts."

"But Olivia expects them to come."

"Why would Olivia request that my daughters come to her party when she accused them of being mean to her and you expressly forbade them playing with her again?" I asked, unable to stop myself taking that particular jab.

"She wants them to come," he reiterated firmly.

"Well, I'm sorry, but Olivia won't be getting what she wants, since we have a prior engagement. Have a lovely day."

Parents today are frightening in their determination not to allow their child to play alone, going so far as to demand play dates and friendships. To those parents, I'd say that, if you want your child to have play dates and friendships, then it's important that her behavior (and yours) reflect friendliness and consideration. If you, or your child, come at people in a demanding manner expecting that everyone will cave to your commands...well, you get the picture: kindness will beget kindness, even if it won't always get you what you want, so be prepared to be let down sometimes, because those you want to be friends with may not have all the time in the world to dedicate to your happiness.

Scenario #3: My daughter and her friend were at the park one afternoon. A little girl, about age five, wanted to play with them. She was a little young to be playing with an eleven- and twelve-year-old, but they acquiesced and played for a little while before deciding to move to a different part of the play area. They thanked the little girl for playing and started to move away, but the little girl started to follow them. They then told her that they were done playing for now.

The little girl began to demand they play with her saying, "Why aren't you playing with me? I want to play a game!"

My daughter told her that they didn't want to play anymore, and the little girl got furious, yelling, "If you don't play with me, I'm not going to be your friend and your being mean to me." She then approached my daughter's friend and started pulling and pushing on his shirt and hitting at him. When he didn't react, she approached my daughter with the intent to do the same thing. My daughter mimicked me and gave her a stern look that said, "That isn't appropriate!" The little girl walked away and went off to cry to her granddad.

Had this girl not been taught that "playing" is a requirement; that she is permitted to play with whomever she chooses for as long as she wants, she would not have behaved this way. She was also mimicking some very aggressive behaviors from someone.

Too often today, parents are setting the wrong tone for playing with other children. It's almost as if it's an expectation; a requirement. As an educator, I understand the importance of socialization. After all, we are trying desperately to weed out bullying and prejudices within a nation of diversity. Yet we must remain cognizant of the fact that not everyone is going to get to play with every person all the time, and for parents to demand it be so is rather petulant. In order for our children to grow up as reasonable adults, they must first be in the company of reasonable adults.

Next, we're going to discuss our pre-teens and teenagers; however, there are many traits common in this age bracket that mirror toddlers and children, so it may seem as if you're reading a lot of what you've already read. There may also be behaviors displayed by *parents*…well, you'll see what I mean.

PART 4: Prepare to be hated

Pre-teens/Teenagers

This lovely group of individuals get a section all of their own, because, while they certainly carry a lot of traits as their younger counterparts (i.e. temper tantrums), those traits advance to a whole other level around the age of twelve. This is mainly because their bodies are changing, raging with unfamiliar hormones. Add to that the changes in their physical bodies due to puberty, and you have a recipe for explosions and meltdowns on a monumental scale. Included within this volatile mixture is peer pressure and influences which compete with your family's morals and values.

Dealing with teenagers will often leave you feeling as if you're on a tightrope, a hundred feet off the ground, with heavy winds, blindfolded and without a balance bar. Tricky proposition, at best.

During this six-year stretch, you'll hear such lovely phrases as: "You just don't get it!" "My life is over!" "No one will ever love me!" "I hate you!" (Thus far, none of mine have shouted the latter, and they swear up and down that they've never even thought it. That's fine by me).

You would think that, if you take the time to consistently train and discipline your child through this time in their lives (preferably beginning at birth), that the teenage years will be smooth sailing. I wish I could say that's fact, but unfortunately, this is the time in your life when the storms are just getting started, because your darling teenager is on their way to becoming an adult; and en route they will begin to test and buck against everything you've ever taught them. Why? Aside from the aforementioned hormones, they are also attempting to find their own identity. Thus, everything you've taught them will come into question, as they question life, love, and societal norms.

Moreover, they will completely overlook the fact that their parents were once teens too. Here are some of the déjà vu moments you'll face once your child hits that special age:

#1—Temper tantrums. I did say that teens have a lot of similar traits to their younger counterparts; however, while children under eleven may suffer tantrums due to being misunderstood, not getting their way, or out of frustration, teens…wait! These are precisely why teenagers throw temper tantrums.

A. *Being misunderstood, or what they perceive as a misunderstanding.* You can provide a logical, rational reason in offering a solution and be faced with a major meltdown. Why? Because it isn't what they want to hear. What they want is for you to empathize and give them what they want. Here's an example:

"Mom, there's this face cleanser that my friend uses. She had acne far worse than me, and it's starting to clear up."

"Your skin has improved a great deal…"

"No, it hasn't! My face is covered in pimples!"

"Okay, but in order to truly make a difference in your skin long term, we need to treat the underlying cause. Cleaning…"

"I do clean it! Every night. And the cleanser you bought just doesn't work!"

"Okay, and drinking plenty of water…"

"I do drink water. You just don't see me; and I'd drink more water here at home if I didn't have to drink that icky tap water. Mom! I need this other cleanser. You just don't understand."

A few dozen pages ago, I mentioned a familiar phrase: *choosing your battles*. This is one of those scenarios in which *choose your battles* comes into play. I could have denied her an expensive cleanser because I know there are ways to combat pimples; however, I chose not to drag the discussion on further, since she'd all but made up her mind anyway. Instead, I told her…

"You earned your own money babysitting, so if you want to purchase this facial product, there isn't any reason why you shouldn't be able to. It's a good thing to spend your money on."

B. *Being interrupted*. We instituted a rule not long ago (still working on making it habit—for all of us), in which the girls will spend a minimum of fifteen minutes a night on tidying their room. This way, it stays clean. Still, remember *timing*. Well, I learned this one the fun way, when I went into one of my daughter's room and said, "Don't forget to take fifteen minutes to tidy your room."

"Mom! I'm right in the middle of writing an essay. If I stop now, I'll lose my train of thought. I have too much homework…"

Oh dear! There comes the meltdown. I quietly waited for her to finish her explosion and then said, "Just remember, please, to take fifteen minutes before bedtime. Thank you." Then I shut the door and returned downstairs. *Sigh*.

Just because a teen has difficulty controlling their emotional outbursts, doesn't mean we should. By taking a deep breath and quietly reiterating what we need them to do, we are teaching them the proper way to interact with others. Which leads to another common trait—arguing.

#2—Fighting or arguing with your teen. I could have included this in the toddler and children section also, because some parents will engage in a battle of words with children as young as three. Okay, I must provide an example here of this, because it really is absurd:

A few years ago, a parent of a then three-year-old dropped her child off and exclaimed in an exasperated tone, "She's one tough cookie to get around." In my head I'm thinking, *she's only three, how tough could she be?*

The parent then explained that earlier that morning she'd gotten into about ten arguments with her daughter because she didn't want to do anything her mother asked her to. This is the same mother that believes being permissive, and being her daughter's best friend, are the way to rear a child. It's also the same mother who called her daughter "feral" and complained every day that her life was a living hell. Enough said.

Anyway, since a teen's brain isn't developed yet, their arguments may seem rational, but because they aren't rational, you won't be able to win a battle with them because it won't matter what you say—their unformed brains will twist and turn and shape it into something other than what you mean. Of course, some adults do the same thing. So, then, how do we combat the urge to argue?

A. Know what you want to communicate and select your *timing*. Sometimes this isn't the most convenient method, because it may never seem a good time for a child or teen, but we can't always wait for them to want to hear us. Still, if you've set aside a certain time of day for play or games, allow them to finish that set-aside time. Don't give directives when it's their allotted time. If you do, and then expect them to hear or not argue with your instruction—it's your own fault. So, if you want to communicate with your child that it's chore time, wait for them to complete their game time and then calmly issue your instructions, using your "please" and "thank you".

B. Remember to phrase your words with manners and in a manner which doesn't allow for decision-making or arguments: "Please ensure that you put your dish in the dishwasher. Thank you". How are they going to argue with that? Well, they may try, but, as the parent—and the adult—we're simply going to reiterate our instruction: "Please ensure that you put your dish in the dishwasher. Thank you. I need to start it soon." By not engaging in a verbal altercation with our child, we are expressing our expectations and demonstrating the proper method in which to speak to others.

There are plenty of times when I'm screaming in my head because my daughters would argue with God himself over something—or try to. Still, while I allow myself the luxury of a mental meltdown within my head, I do my utmost to prevent that from being displayed outwardly. In fact, I used to tell my children, related to arguing with me, that "if I say the sky is black, you say 'yes ma'am'. The only time you're allowed to argue with me is if someone's life is in danger."

C. Avoid permissive statements. "Can you…" "Would you…" or "Would you like…" statements when you know full well you expect something different, is a recipe for explosions. If you have a specific expectation, make certain that expectation is clearly and politely relayed. For example: "Ensure that you wear your jacket today, please. It's going to be chilly out. Thank you." Again, just because you say it doesn't mean they won't find a way to argue: "I don't need a coat. I'm not cold." Calmly reiterate, "It's going to be chilly today, please ensure you wear your jacket. We don't want you getting sick. Thank you." You are not arguing, you are merely repeating your instruction politely and with a firm tone.

D. Have them repeat the instruction. This is a big one in my book, because there isn't a child on this planet who will listen fully when a parent is speaking, unless it's in their own interest to do so. We call this trait, *listening with half an ear.* But how can not listening lead to arguing? Well, if you think your child heard you and then simply chose to ignore your instruction, you aren't going to be happy. And when you confront your child about it, they're going to argue that they simply didn't hear you. So ensure they do.

One day, in the car, as I pulled up to the house after running errands, I gave my girls an instruction. They both muttered, "Yes ma'am" as they'd been taught, but I wasn't taking any chances.

"Okay, y'all, repeat what I said please."

Sheepishly, one reiterated my instructions, getting half of what I said correct. She'd completely zoned out by the second half. The other one managed to recall precisely the entire instruction (miracles do happen).

To ensure my instruction would be followed, I had them reiterate it one more time, when we got into the house, which garnered a "Mom, we heard you!" response from both. Still, I'd rather not take chances. By doing this, they no longer have an excuse—the biggest of which is, "I didn't hear you!" or "I forgot!" The "I forgot" leads me to the next tactic.

E. Issue the instruction when you know it can be done right then, and then ensure it is done right then. If you allow them the fifteen minutes more to finish their show, or whatever it is they're doing, then they *will* forget, and it's likely you will also. This coincides with timing though, so if you said they could finish a show, don't issue the instruction until that show is finished. If you're worried you'll forget by then, do what I do—make a note.

That works for them also. You can jot it down or have them do so. After you give them the instruction and they repeat it, have it written down, so if they try the "just fifteen minutes more, Mom?" they'll have the reminder in front of them. We adults do something similar, yeah? When we have a ton of things we need to accomplish, we make a list. Well, what's wrong with teaching your children to make a list of things they need to get accomplished in their day?

In addition to the above issues, there will be many ways in which you will disappoint your child, giving them plenty of reasons to hate you. Live with it. You are not here to be their friend you are here to ensure they grow up to be responsible adults. Once they reach adulthood, there can be a paradigm shift to friendship. I tell my children all of the time, "I'm not your friend, I'm your mom. When you get to be eighteen, then we can be friends. In the meantime, it's my responsibility to teach you how to be responsible, hard-working, productive adults."

It's an unpopular viewpoint today in a society which seems to think children should be in charge of their lives, their own education, to make their own decisions, and be their parents' friend. A viewpoint that is creating a generation of entitled-minded, spoiled, irresponsible brats who are incapable of tending to their own needs, who blame everyone else for their mistakes, and can't seem to hold a job. It's as if parents today are afraid to parent.

We were watching an episode of Boston Legal the other night, where a fifteen-year-old girl got pregnant and contracted Aids as a result. Her reaction? To sue the school. Why? Because it was their fault for teaching abstinence and not offering options. Oh, did my husband and I ever have a discussion about *that!* How many things were wrong with this scenario? Let us count the ways:

The girl made the mistake. She could have not gone to a boy's house alone; she could have chosen not to engage in a sexual act. Despite the abstinence only policy, she could have acquired condoms, as she was obviously familiar with them.

Why is it the school's problem? Why are we expecting the educational system to train our children when we are supposed to be doing that at home?

Where were the parents? Why weren't they the ones held responsible, since—at age fifteen—she is still a minor and therefore their responsibility? If they weren't keen on the abstinence only education, they could have easily filled in the gaps and explained other alternatives.

In the end, all this teenager learned was how to make a major mistake, not accept responsibility for that mistake; how to blame someone other than herself and make someone else pay for that mistake.

The only way to change the way things are going now is for parents to step up and actually be parents.

PART 5: Don't be afraid to be the parent

Admittedly, being a parent today takes courage, because there are so many people just waiting for you to screw up so they can report you to child welfare services; so many people saying that you can't discipline or cause your child distress in any way, shape, or form. Different people who are willing to criticize your methods, especially if it differs from their beliefs. Even the methods I discuss in this book will be criticized by those who take issue with my techniques. The good news is—you're the one who brought your children into this world, so it should be you who determines the best method for rearing them. There isn't anything wrong with doing your research or learning from those who've already raised children, but in the end—you're the parent, so don't be afraid to *be* the parent.

Moreover, I have encountered many parents today who are simply afraid to parent. They are scared they'll offend their child; or that their child will grow to dislike them. If you plan to have children, you need to get used to the idea that you're in charge and you have a responsibility to raise that child to be a responsible, productive member of society. To do that, you're going to have to set aside your fear and get past the worries over whether your child will like you or not. You are not their friend; you are their teacher and their mentor. If they dislike you…well, mine still love me and we're quite close. I'm best friends with my oldest children, and I didn't cave and become a fearful, permissive parent to get that relationship. I was a firm parent who had reasonable expectations for her children. They turned out just wonderful. At the end of this book, I'm going to list the current types of parenting. What you want to strive to be is Authoritative.

When a parent told me that she didn't want the Authoritative style of parenting to clash with her ideals, beliefs, love of nature, etc., I simply told her that they didn't have to. It is possible to meld them, with great success. Okay, I digressed, so…

Below are a few areas to assist you on the road to raising your child with grace and dignity.

#1—Choose your battles wisely. As mentioned, a few times already: early in a child's life, you are a dictator (a positive one). You are in charge of and responsible for every aspect of that child's life. You are the decision-maker. Eventually though, you're going to want to start letting the reins loosen a little more with each passing year, so that, when they reach eighteen, they are ready to go off leash into the world; to be successful college students or working adults. The leash loosening generally begins between the age of eight and twelve. Even then, you are still the decision-maker and in charge of every aspect of their life. However, with that being said, you will also allow your child—with guidance—to start making decisions, simpler decisions when on the younger side, developing into more complex decision-making when older. This is where choosing your battles comes in:

Scenario #1:

"Johnny, yours socks don't match. Change them, please. Thank you."

"But, Mom, this is the way all the kids are wearing their socks now."

STOP!

Do we really want to cause a fight over socks? Is that really a life-altering decision? Perhaps it's okay to allow your child to have this concession.

"Very well. I see no reason why not. Finish up quickly, please. We need to leave. Thank you."

Scenario #2:

"Mom, all of my friends are going to the lake this weekend."

"Will there be chaperones?"

"Oh, absolutely!"

"Will there be boys and girls together on this weekend trip?"

"Yes, but I think I'm old enough to make this decision…"

STOP!

This could very well be a life-altering decision, and one that we will not allow our child to make. Why? Because we are still responsible for her welfare; and if she ends up making a rash, irresponsible decision—such as sleeping with a boy because he's declared his undying love for her which leads to her getting pregnant or a communicable disease, or AIDS—you and your daughter will pay the price for allowing that child to make a monumental decision.

But I think there should be a level of trust. After all, I'm raising my child to make their own decisions.

Okay, fair enough, and once their frontal lobe has developed, they *will* be able to make their own decisions; however, until that lobe develops, it's our job to assist in the decision-making process. Remember, the frontal lobe is the central command center in charge of problem-solving, decision-making, rationality, judgement calls, planning, attention span, inhibition (or lack thereof); and until it reaches maturity, your child will make irrational, ill-planned, ill-conceived decisions and be prone to rash actions because they think they're invincible. Trust has nothing to do with it.

So, the rule of thumb for gradually allowing decision-making is to gauge the potential consequences. If the consequences will not cause potential harm to your child, consider allowing them the decision. It will build their confidence in their abilities. If the decision has the potential to harm, then step up and be the parent. They may not like you for it, but they will thank you for it down the road.

#2—Contrary to what they say, children do not know everything. Have you ever started to explain something to your child, only to have them interrupt with an "I know" followed by that irritating eye roll? This actually happened to me recently with one of my daycare children. I noticed that she was starting to put her shoe on the wrong foot, so told her so, to which she responded, "I know" and rolled her eyes. It was the first time this four-year-old toddler had ever done anything of that sort, so I was taken aback initially. I know she hadn't picked it up from me or my girls, because my children hadn't even come close to attempting the "I know eye roll" for more years than which I've been in business. I hid the grin that tried to form on my mouth (it really was comical) and affected my stern face and stern tone, "Young lady, it is not respectful for you to do what you did, so we're going to use caution in future". She immediately (instinctively) said, "Yes, Mrs. Barbara" (she knows my tones).

Still, if you haven't had children yet, or if your children are still really young, be expecting it because it's coming.

For such small human beings who haven't been on the planet all that many years, some children really seem to have the impression they know everything, or at least more than their parents…and in some cases, it's the parents fault.

Whoa! What did she just say?

I said that, in some cases, it's the parents fault. Here's an example:

I know a man who raised his son to be very independent and proved a prodigy in one particular area. That son also turned out to be a wise-ass and a know-it-all, because his dad would say things like, "Oh, my son is a lot smarter than I am." "Oh, my son had to teach me a thing or two about this." "If I need help with this particular thing, I ask my son." Well, that son started hearing that from about age five, so needless to say, by the time he was fifteen, he had no need of parents because, after all, he was smarter than them. Forget that his frontal lobe hadn't finished developing yet—so while he may have been a prodigy in a particular area, his parents still had things to educate him on regarding life in general. Even prodigies have a frontal lobe that still needs to finalize development.

Still, some children use the "I know eye-roll" as a deflection because they simply don't want to hear what their parents have to say. Do they really think they know everything? No— and they really don't. So, we, as parents, can get frustrated by the "I know" syndrome, or we can simply continue to educate our child until they really *do* know.

Should we allow them to get away with rolling their eyes when we speak? Obviously not. After all, it's generally regarded as an act of disrespect. Do you think that if you rolled your eyes at your boss, he would simply overlook it? Of course not. Well, we parents are the boss in our home, and we need to ensure our child learns respectful behavior.

Still, remember that every action we address needs to be done in a positive, calm manner. Would your boss yell at you or hit you over the head for being disrespectful? Not likely. Well, when your child rolls his or her eyes, try remembering that you're their boss: "Sam, when we're talking, it's disrespectful to roll our eyes. Let's make an effort to cease that behavior, or they'll need to be consequences."

#3 -- If you don't know the answer, don't be afraid to say, "Let's look it up". You notice I didn't say to reply, "I don't know." Remember, you're supposed to be the wise one; the one to whom your little one is going to look up to; to come to for answers. So, what do you think will happen if you say, "I don't know" to a question?

Well, we should let our children see our weaknesses; we should let them know we're human and don't know everything. Okay, you run with that, and before long your children will be seeking answers from someone who's not afraid to give them answers—even if they're the wrong answers.

In reality, we are their Superheroes, and the moment they discover we aren't as smart as we are supposed to be or we prove infallible, their little world will begin to crumble. There will come a day, when they are older and wiser and able to stand on their own two feet (after their frontal lobe develops fully), when we can begin to allow them to see our frailties (in small doses). We don't have to, but by then, they'll be better able to cope with it.

So, if we're supposed to be Superheroes who know everything, how do we get around the fact that we *don't* know everything? We use the guise of teaching them how to research their own answers; and in a world where answers are virtually at our fingertips, this method is even easier than when I was little.

I would love to take credit for this marvelous idea, but I can't. The credit goes to a former teacher of mine, long, long ago in a middle school far, far away. If we were working on a project and asked her a question, she would say, "This library is full of books, so look it up. If you need assistance, I'm right here." I'm now a master of research and if ever I have a question, I look it up. I use the same tactic with my children, often assisting in the process because I want them to understand how to look things up on the internet safely and effectively. Keeping them safe, after all, is my job also.

The pitfalls of revealing your weaknesses too soon can be demonstrated in the following anecdote. This person was not a parent, rather a teacher, and her response to a query I made one day will stay with me forever; especially as she was my student-teaching mentor and someone to whom I was supposed to look up to, admire, and respect.

She couldn't spell all that well. Concerned over the fact that she was teaching the children how to spell words incorrectly, I asked if *she* wasn't concerned about it. Her reply, "No, I think the children should see our faults; that they should see us make mistakes. It puts us closer to their level."

Hmm. But I thought we were supposed to be educating them to be above that current level? I thought. To her, however, I replied, "I have to respectfully disagree. As teachers, we should be setting an example on the importance of education."

"Well, if it bothers you that much, you're a good speller. I'll just send the kids over to you when they ask to spell something." And she did; and so did the two other teachers on the team. Apparently, there's a trend among some teachers today, where spelling and grammar are not high priorities (My children and I have met quite a few), but that's a soapbox topic for another book.

I wondered how the children felt about the teacher's inability to spell so I asked them one day, to which one replied, "Why should I care? If I can't spell, I'll just become a teacher too." Oh, joy!

Here was an individual who was supposed to be a Superhero; was supposed to be infallible in the eyes of little ones (and in my eyes), but who allowed her flaws to shine through as if it was a badge of honor; not realizing that she was losing the respect of her students and her student-teacher. Do we really want to lose the respect of our children because we think it is okay to pretend they're smarter than we are, or to show our flaws before they're ready to accept them? If you don't know something—look it up. It's better than saying, "I don't know" a thousand times over, and will teach your child an invaluable skill in the process—how to conduct research.

And, if you really don't know, consider joining in the research with your child; or tell them, "let me know what you find out." Doing this engages your child in your life more. By sharing his or her research, you learn something new and you get to spend time with your child that will prove invaluable.

When a couple of my children became adults, I said "I don't know" to a query once, and they nearly fell off their chairs in shock. It was quite comical. I then said, "Hey, now would be a good time to learn. Let's look it up!" They recovered their even keel quickly and we did just that. Slowly they discovered that sometimes even momma needs to look things up.

#3—Learn to communicate openly and honestly with your child. Sex, Drugs, Alcohol, Bullying, Sharing, Kindness, Friendship…some of these topics we begin talking to our children about the minute they exit the womb; others, we shy away from because the topics are too embarrassing to think about, or we believe our child will rise above the crowd and not participate in activities that will shame his or her family.

Oh, yes, they will, and if we don't communicate with them, address their curiosities openly and honestly, they are going to get their information from someone or somewhere less reliable; someone who doesn't have their best interest at heart; someone who may not know anything but is willing to impart his or her stupidity. Need I go on?

This gets tricky though, because instead of being honest and imparting the facts, some parents take the opportunity to scare their children straight, hoping that the fear of a thing will keep their children from experimenting later. In reality, think back through history—things that were taught as taboo, ended up being the very thing that kids wanted to try: drinking, cigarettes, drugs, sex… *Why is this taboo? What makes it so scary?* Remember, it is better to be honest and direct, answering questions as they arise, rather than generating a mystery in which children find a need to solve that mystery.

Some of the questions I've encountered from my own children as young as eight, range from curiosity over sex to having babies, to questions about drinking, drugs, and alcohol. If you aren't certain about a topic, or it's embarrassing to discuss—look it up or go to the experts.

My mom took me and my sisters to a nurse when she was ready to discuss sex and reproduction, where we were provided full-color charts and statistics; where we were able to speak to someone qualified to answer all our curiosities. There are thousands of websites, many managed by experts, where you can find answers related to many of your child's questions. The trick is to ensure you locate a reliable source, and no, that wouldn't be Wikipedia.

If you provide your child direct, honest, and *complete* information related to a topic, then they will be better prepared when peer pressure attempts to lead them astray. They will have all the information they need to make informed decisions when they are grown and no longer beneath the umbrella of your care. They also will know that no matter how old they get, you will always be there as someone they can turn to; someone they can trust; someone who will provide them honest, reliable answers to their questions.

So, if you talk to you children when they come to you and ask something, they are more likely to seek your council when something confusing arises. Here's an example:

My daughters spent time in the company of a young girl a couple of years their senior. Early on, she often made outlandish claims which would have the girls knitting their brows in confusion. Had I not been available to correct this young lady's uninformed and incorrect information, my children could very well have taken this older child's word as fact. Now, a few years later, they know to take this girl's word with a grain of salt.

Do I need worry now that this girl will be able to talk my children into smoking, drinking, or playing hooky from school? Not in the least. Not because of trust, rather because I discredited the source well enough, with honest facts, that they would prefer to rely on my judgement than that of a sixteen-year-old.

Remember, in order to remain a positive influence on your children, you must be a positive influence. When I say to talk to your children openly and honestly, I also mean factually.

Too often, parents allow their prejudices to taint fact, which is why racism, hatred, fear, teen pregnancy and drug use still run rampant today.

#4—Children of all ages need structure. This particular topic goes hand-in-hand with consistency, balance, and scheduling. Just as discipline needs consistency and balance, so does a child's day. Not only will this afford balance and serve as a calming tactic; it will also prepare them for life: from the first day of school when they'll be following a scheduled routine; to entering the work force, when schedules will be a part of life. Even if you only schedule mealtimes and game time, that's better than leaving the day up-in-the-air all the time.

For my daycare, routine (structure) is part of their day. They know, when they walk in, they are to sit on the stairwell, remove their shoes and put it in the shoe area; they know to immediately move to the play area after hugging and kissing their parents goodbye (that's required ☺). They are so familiar with snack time and mealtime, that as soon as I move to feed a younger child, the older ones pipe up, "We'll eat as soon as the younger ones are fed." The children in my facility have a sense of structure, which lends an air of security and safety—something all children need to feel.

What happens if we have an appointment that disrupts our routine? Life is full of disruptions, which affords the opportunity to discuss with your child what to do if their day is disrupted, to teach calming methods. So that when they grow up and that alarm clock doesn't go off, they won't panic. Instead, they will know that they need to get going as soon as is possible and to inform their boss of the delay.

Life doesn't go according to plan, which is why we need to give our children every tool available to make it as livable as possible.

PART 6: Raising an independent and responsible child

Every day is an educational opportunity

#1—Education begins at home. When I say this, I'm not just referring to academics, rather to every aspect of life. If you treat every opportunity as a learning experience, then your child will gain valuable knowledge which they may not even realize you were teaching them. Still, academics are also a parental responsibility. Don't wait until your child heads to school for them to start learning. Give them a leg up. Even a trip to the park can offer an opportunity to teach mathematics or science: "Oh my goodness, there are so many ducks out today. I wonder how many there are. Think we can count them all?" or "The leaves sure are green. Can you tell me why you think they're green?" A ride in the car to the grocery store can provide an excellent chance for a spelling lesson: "There's a sign coming up. Let's see how many words you can read or spell on that sign." Believe it or not, engaging your child in such a fashion will also lessen the opportunities they have for bickering and fighting, which may just save your sanity.

Other opportunities for teaching life lessons are going to be obvious. For example, I use television shows and movies as an opening to engage my children. Oftentimes, after watching a movie, I will ask, "What did that teach you? Good or bad?" You'd be surprised at what they pick up, and the opening it gives you to set the record straight, or to concur with a positive message.

I'm sorry, but I work two jobs just to earn enough to survive. I don't have time to teach my children. That's what schools are for. I certainly can empathize. I was a single parent once upon a time and know how difficult it is to balance children, job(s), emotional upheavals, stress—*life*. But what I learned was that I could make life a positive example—including working hard—or I could shut my children out and rely on someone else to raise them for me. It takes a serious mental shift and pushing back exhaustion; but if you can just spare your child half hour a day to teach them to read or write or to appreciate education at all, then there will be less struggle as they grow up. I give you my word.

#2—Teach your child to be a "try hard". I can't take credit for this little motivator. My daughter said that it started spreading around her school one year; but I can appreciate the message. The one I use at home is similar. I tell my children (related to academics): "Try your best and the grades will follow". *Well, what if that grade is a "C"?* (I told you they'll always find a way to argue). If your child did their best and obtained a "C", perhaps the subject matter was tougher than even a "try hard" could master. Do we criticize and berate the letter grade, or do we positively motivate them to do a bit of extra research to help learn more about the topic they're struggling with? Motivating them to "try hard" and to find ways to improve, will only serve them constructively when they enter the work force. How? Let's say their boss assigns them a project, but they're uncertain of how best to complete that project. Knowing how to tackle a difficult task and do the research needed to form comprehension will give them the confidence needed to do their best.

It doesn't mean they'll always succeed, but it does communicate that things are not going to always be easy; that effort is required. Often times, people search for the easy way or the fast way, which often results in sloppy or shoddy work—in academics and in the workplace. Teaching them to respect what they do—to be a "try hard"—will give them the start needed to make success more probable than not.

#3—Good work ethics equals…. Earlier I stated that one of the discussions you should have with your spouse is whether you're pro-chores or anti-chores? Well, this next section is going to reveal that I am pro-chores—big time.

From the moment my children could walk, they would help me to push the vacuum cleaner around the house; I would give them a baby wipe to help "clean"; they would pick up and put away their toys. All of these were an introduction to the importance of teaching a good work ethic. If children learn—even through fun, participatory activities—that work is a part of life, they are less likely to go into shock when they enter school and discover homework is a chore; they are less likely to balk when you tell them it's time to get a job.

But my two-year-old doesn't need to do chores. She's too young. Is she too young to make a mess? Of course not. And if you teach her that mommy or daddy is there to clean up her mess—all the time—then when you finally get around to the idea that she's old enough to clean up her own mess, your little princess is going to fight against it, tooth and nail; screams and wails. Then the battles are on and training your child will become a war that will last longer than World War II did (that battle lasted six years).

However, if you begin instruction before they realize that chores actually involve work, it simply becomes habit, a way of life. Does starting early mean that your children will do a chore happily whistling a tune, all the time? Good Lord, no! They're still going to balk. I swear, every time I tell my daughters it's time to empty the dishwasher, neither do so without accompanying whines and wails. I'm convinced that whining and moaning are simply their way of expressing how they feel about doing it. They do it though, and they know it's their chore to do. We adults don't go about our daily work with a smile all of the time either, but we do it just the same.

When the girls got older, we sometimes preceded chores with a game; an actual game, such as Rummy or Uno. Whoever won, got first choice from a list. Second place, got second choice, etc. Often the game lasted an hour, so that each person had an opportunity to win a first selection after each round of play. In whichever manner you decide to allot chores, doing so will ensure that when they grow up, they aren't likely to forget that dishes need to be washed, floors vacuumed or mopped, counters cleaned, or toilets scrubbed. It will simply be a part of life, complaints notwithstanding.

You aren't their bank

As with chores, parents need to discuss whether their child will receive an allowance; and as with chores, I'm pro-allowance. What I'm not keen on, is the idea of simply handing money over without a reason. I'm not a bank. I work for my money, and I expect my children to learn that same concept. (This excludes birthdays and Christmas gifts). My dad used to tell us that, if we earned our money and then paid for our own things, we learned to respect that money and the things we bought.

So, as long as they are completing given chores (whining or not), they get "a paycheck". I then try to encourage them to "spend" that paycheck responsibly, and also to "save" part of that paycheck towards bigger ticket items that they are interested in (i.e. bicycles) or towards "retirement". Yes, even a child as early as two can be taught the importance of money and how to earn, spend, and save it responsibly. Start early, and perhaps when they arrive at retirement age, they won't have to rely on a Social Security system that may have collapsed by then.

I simply don't earn enough money to give them anything. This may prove an unpopular suggestion, but I'm going to make it. If you purchased just one less bag of chips, latte, pack of cigarettes, hamburger, beer, book, or t-shirt…just one less…you could not only save your own money, but it would provide a dollar or two a week for your child to learn proper spending and saving habits. No one said that an allowance had to equate to an actual adult paycheck.

Not certain where your money is going, so are uncertain where you can pull an extra dollar or two from? Try keeping track for a few months; making a budget. Not only is this a positive habit for adults to engage in regularly it also provides a positive example for children to follow. If children learn to comprehend that money is not infinite; that what they earn is limited based on what they must spend that money on, then they will learn to value money.

Responsible spending habits

Expecting children to earn their money, goes hand-in-hand with teaching them the best way to spend that money. If we allow them to take their allowance down to the candy store and blow it all on treats, not only are we teaching them to burn through their cash, but also poor eating and purchasing habits. So then, do we deny them that candy? Personally, I don't have a problem with treats; however, we should teach them to divvy up that cash and spend it on different things, save it for better things. Some things, however, would take forever for a child to earn, so I used to have a method for saving for those expensive things that my children "really wanted", such as a PlayStation or a bicycle.

I would tell them that if they were able to save up half the cost, I would cover the other half (which meant that I needed to save too). That way, they learned to save, but didn't have to wait a lifetime.

Responsibility and consequences

I touched on this a little earlier, but here I would love to expound upon the importance of educating our children to accept responsibility and the consequences for one's actions. Whether good or bad, everything in life that we do, will have positive or negative consequences, and will affect everyone around us. There is never anything that we will do that will not impact someone else.

Moreover, it is imperative that we teach our children to accept responsibility for everything they do, whether the resulting consequence is good or bad. Too often today, I'll sit down and watch the local news and see example after example of people who cannot accept responsibility. Here are just a few stories I've borne witness to and had to shake my head as a result:

1. A man gets angry while driving home. The car behind him honks, so the man's response is to get out and shoot him. Who's to blame for this atrocity? Well, according to the shooter, it was the man who honked the horn at him.

2. A teenager joins a gang and shoots a rival gang member. When cornered by the police, he tries to shoot his way out and is gunned down in the process. Who's to blame for the boy's death? Well, according to the distraught mother being interviewed by the local networks—everyone *but* her son. Her son was a "good boy" who got mixed up with the "wrong crowd" and wouldn't "hurt a flea". Well, um, he did.

3. A lady, who's convinced the leash laws don't apply to her, allows her dog to wander the neighborhood. The dog runs into the road during one of their walks and gets struck by a car. Who's to blame? According to the dog owner, it's the driver of the car.

Still, let's back the drama down a notch and deal with our own children. Here are some instances in which parents have refused to allow their child to take responsibility:

1. A boy throws a baseball through a neighbor's window, but instead of the parents offering to pay for the window, they declare, "It was just an accident."

2. A child, playing catch in the street near parked cars, dents someone's door. Instead of the parent making the boy apologize and offering to pay for the repairs, the parent says, "Prove it was my son."

These are just a few of the incidences that occur on a daily basis, but there was a positive occurrence also that happened not too long ago.

A teenager driving home late at night, skirted too close to *my* car and broke the review mirror. Instead of "getting away with it", he stopped, wrote a note, and placed it beneath my windshield wiper. The next day, his father stopped by to apologize and to give me his insurance information. They remained in constant communication until the situation was resolved. The parent even required his son to pay anything over that which the insurance didn't cover. Despite the consequences being negative, this parent showed his child how to accept responsibility for what he'd done. Now *that* is great parenting in action.

Do you think that responsible behavior evolved all on its own? Of course not. It was the result of training. In our home, when a child breaks something through negligent behavior or from breaking a house rule (i.e. playing catch indoors), then they are required to use their allowance to replace or repair the broken item. Fortunately, this happened infrequently and not in recent memory. No child wants to lose their money, so will learn caution fairly quick if made to literally "pay" for their mistakes.

Be a shepherd not a sheep

A shepherd is the leader, the person whom sheep follow; the sheep, though adorable animals, will follow that shepherd to their death; to become lamb chops on someone's table. Nothing wrong with that—if you're a sheep—but when it comes to our children, do we want them to be sheep? Following a poor example of a person to their death in a gang shoot out? Do we want them to land in jail because they blindly followed a stronger personality in committing a crime? Do we want them to be sheep, incapable of being the leader of their household, a positive example whom their children can emulate?

Of course not. We want them to be the shepherd. The kindly individual whom the sheep follow. In order to ensure that our children become shepherds and not sheep, we must teach them to be positive, brave, intelligence-seeking, answer-finders, courageous-doers. We must give them the skills to become responsible, successful adults. Only then can we be assured that we, as parents, have done right by our child.

I'm a Christian but wanted to ensure that this book related to anyone raising children; however, I feel compelled to address an issue that some Christians, reading this book may balk at, stating that Jesus was the Shepherd and we're his sheep. In religious circumstances, following Christ is not related to the shepherd to sheep context I'm referring to in raising children in the world today. The context I'm referring to is that our children should be strong, independent, responsible, capable adults whom others wish to emulate, so hold off on the letters of reprimand, please. Thank you. ☺

Finances

Educating your child on being a good steward of their finances is essential in ensuring they remain successful adults. It goes along with training them how to spend and save their allowance; but as they get older, we also need to teach them about the differences, the importance, and the pitfalls of bank accounts, credit cards, debit cards, loans, and other areas of finance.

A good start, as mentioned briefly earlier, is to teach your child the importance of a budget. If you can teach your child how to gauge what's coming in with what's going out, they can learn to respect their earnings and know its limitations.

Just as with any other area of life, knowledge of responsible finances isn't something a child learns unassisted. It is taught—and the people who are supposed to do the teaching, should be the parents, through both example and instruction.

A good beginning is to open your child a savings account as soon as permissible by your banking institution. Then, teach them how to contribute a portion of their allowance to that account on a regular basis. With this can come lessons on interest accumulation.

As they get older and obtain their first part time job, open a fiduciary checking account for them. You are a partner on that account, so that you can keep tabs on how things are going. After all, you can't instruct if you're blind to your child's spending habits.

If you're all for obtaining a credit card, assist them locating one with a reasonable rate and teach them how it works, interest rates, what happens if they miss a monthly payment, and what credit cards are meant to be (a source for emergencies only). Ensure that you get this for them while they are still in your home so that you can monitor usage, payments, and reel in the propensity to go wild because they don't quite comprehend that a credit card is a loan that must be repaid.

PART 7: Stop fretting over EVERYTHING

Am I a bad mom if I don't volunteer; don't bake; don't do crafts?

I actually asked myself these questions quite a few times in my youth, because I was not one of those moms who was drawn to arts and crafts, spending time in the kitchen baking, and I was working too hard just to survive to take the time to volunteer. I made up for it all by taking my time off to play and read with my children.

When they were old enough to be in the kitchen, I would have them join me, so they could start learning to cook, training them. Now, my two youngest (just barely into their teens) cook their own meals most times. I wanted to ensure, just as I did with their older sisters, that they would be able to feed themselves properly when they left my home. So, do I feel guilty that I am not Susie-Homemaker-Super Baker? No! My children still learned a valuable skill and spent time with Momma.

As for volunteering. While I truly wished I had more time for this service, I simply don't. I can't allow myself to feel guilty for holding a job and supporting my children; nor can my husband. We do what we are supposed to do—work and support our family. Am I missing out on anything? No. Because I have communication skills that I've taught my children, so every day while dinner is cooking or just after getting home from school, the girls regale me with their day.

If you are a stay-at-home-mom (a job in and of itself) and you have the opportunity to volunteer at your child's school, I do hope you take that opportunity. Our schools are in dire need of help in many areas and would benefit from the knowledge and skills you bring to the classroom.

Am I a bad dad if my son prefers dance to sports?

Try not to fret over this too much. Not every child is going to grow up a football player. Still, if sports mean that much to you, simply introduce your child to them early on. If they take to a sport, so be it. If they appear to prefer a different avenue...my recommendation is to allow it. It's your child's happiness, not yours.

One thing you're going to encounter as your child searches for something he or she prefers—activity jumping. They are going to begin karate, decide they aren't really that fond of it, and request to try piano, decide they aren't really fond of it, and then request to start football...

There are two trains of thought on this:

1) We should teach our child to finish something they start; and 2) We shouldn't pressure our child to do something they don't like.

I'm kind of on the fence on this one. I think we should teach a child to stick with something, so that they are better able to hold down a job when it gets difficult. I'm also fond of not pressuring a child into doing something they aren't fond of—if it's not life related. Sports or other similar activities are not going to determine whether our child can hold a job or not, so if they decide they aren't fond of football, have them complete a full term—to satisfy teaching them to complete something—and then allow them to test something else out. Eventually, something will click and the light in their eyes when you say, "It's time to head to cricket practice" will be worth the flexibility.

Technology: It's all about balance

Technology is here, and it's here to stay. That's a fact. What I find interesting however, is parents' reticence to allow their child to engage in technology because they are becoming too obsessed with it? One thing I hear frequently is: "I don't think we should allow our children to play video games or use an iPad because we are teaching them how *not* to play." When one person told me this, I replied:

"Actually, children need to be introduced to technology early and as much as possible, because our work force, and the work force of the future, is technology driven, and those with the knowledge will be successful in future. To me, it's no different than a farmer teaching his child the trade of farming. That farmer is going to ensure his son knows how to work with a tractor and other equipment to make certain he has the tools to be successful; the tools he'll need to support a family. He'll do this in conjunction with the requisite lessons on safety. Technology is no different. Taught in balance with playtime and other life essentials (including lessons on safe usage), our children will become capable technology users."

To those parents who allow their children to watch television eight hours a day; or to sit at the dinner table and text…your child is not learning balance, which is probably why you're anti-technology. Our daughters have a cell phone, which they barely touch; a Kindle, which they play on when they don't have homework, chores, or are told to play outdoors; a computer, which they primarily use to complete homework assignments. Their life is balanced, and technology is a part of that balance.

There's another thing I've heard said: "Technology is evil". That would make technology a person. Inanimate objects can't be evil. People *can* be. Which is why I'm always amazed (and a bit distressed) when people attach an action to an object instead of the person using that object. Guns aren't evil, people are, computers aren't evil, people are…and with people comes the potential to misuse any inanimate object. My husband said something to me related to this that I found very profound. He said, "Human beings are the only creature on the planet with the potential to be the worst or the best at anything." No other animal on the planet has that potential because no other animal is sentient, capable of rational or irrational thought.

Foods / Feeding

The latest in a long line of food worries is allergies and organics.

Organics. People jumped on board this latest development faster than any other I've seen in my lifetime. Many were guilted into it, while others truly find organic foods a positive alternative. No matter your stance on organic food, do your research, determine its impact on your budget, and make up your own mind. I can assure you, without reservation that your child will survive if they don't eat everything organic. I did, and my children have. All of us are healthy and happy and haven't suffered any ill effects paying a few dollars less for our food. If you can afford to eat organic, and really feel there's a benefit, then go for it. Whatever you do, don't stress over it. If your decision is yours, own it.

Food allergies. The fretting over foods and what a child should or should not consume has led to an all-time high in food related allergies. Children who survived eons eating cheese and peanut butter, now break out in hives or suffer life-threatening reactions just being in the vicinity of either. Could there be a medical reason? Some doctors say yes. Since I'm not an expert, here's some expert information to help take the worry out of why your child is suffering from allergies today that we never even considered when we were a child. Is this meant to cause concern? Absolutely not. If your child is not predisposed to outbreaks or allergies (mine aren't), it isn't likely they're going to develop them just because you're reading the potential exists, so breathe and keep reading:

"When a baby is born, its immune system is a work in progress. "You're born with a naïve, allergic-skewed immune system," explains Dr. Michael Cyr, an allergist and immunologist at McMaster University in Hamilton, Ontario. This is what scientists call the Th2 mode.

During the first days, weeks and months of life, as the baby comes into contact with various germs, bacteria, viruses and infection, the system is supposed to start learning to distinguish between what is harmful and what is benign.

Some allergists liken the emerging immune system to a toggle switch or a reset button: we're all born in that Th2 mode and then that first bout of sniffles at eight weeks or the ear infection at four months begins to "switch" the immune system over from Th2 to Th1 mode or fighting bacterial infection mode.

But in the person with a genetic inclination to allergy, something misfires and the switchover doesn't happen properly. Cyr, who's a researcher with AllerGen (the Allergy, Genes and Environment Network), says that why this process happens easily for some people but not for others remains unclear, and may depend on a confluence of factors.

The young child who doesn't get switched over is now atopic—predisposed to developing an allergic response to a trigger such as cat dander or ragweed pollen or peanuts. After breathing in or consuming one of those, the child's immune system creates allergy antibodies—specifically Immunoglobulin E or IgE antibodies—to guard against the offending trigger. The next time the immune system encounters it, the IgE will go on the defensive, setting off a cascade of allergic symptoms.

Though genetics are a large contributing factor to whether a person becomes allergic, scientists haven't found one specific allergy gene. "It's becoming clear that it's not a gene, it's a whole series of genes," says Cyr. Something has changed to increase the number of us who are developing allergies, says Dr. Dennis Ownby, a professor of pediatrics and the head of allergy and immunology at the Medical College of Georgia in Augusta.

In our modern world, allergy has spread like wildfire. Scientists are certain that genes alone can't be the whole reason why. "The genetic pool does not dramatically change over decades," notes Cyr. "So it's obvious there's something else going on." And that something appears to be our environment.

Apparently, some children, born in certain environments—particularly highly pollutant environments—are more prone to develop allergies over those whose environments are less polluted. So, the next time we wonder why so many children today are developing allergies to foods that generations prior never suffered from, we can surmise that they either developed a weak immune system or live in a highly polluted environment. Neither of which is a pleasant thought, but at least it provides us a clue.

Shedding light on anything unfamiliar is a good way to take away the intimidation factor. Knowledge is power, after all.

Injuries

From the moment children learn to crawl, and especially to walk, they are going to fall down go boom. How we, as parents, handle those moments, will determine whether our child grows into strong, capable adults or fearful, neurotic hypochondriacs. Too harsh? Maybe, but true.

Here are two examples:

Little Eric and Tommy are playing on the playground. They fall from the play structure (about a foot off the ground). Eric's mom strolls over, gives him the once over (to check for injury), brushes off the dirt, gives him a quick kiss on the head and then shoos him off, "You're okay, sweetheart. Go play."

Tommy's mom immediately starts screeching, tearing across the playground as if her child just fell from a ten-story building. "Tommy! Tommy! Are you okay? Oh, my God, let me check. Does anything hurt? Is anything bleeding? Maybe we need to go to the doctor. You might have a concussion." Tommy, who initially didn't think twice about the fall, and was more than ready to go back to playing, now bursts into tears. Why? One of two reasons: 1) his mother's antics scared the tar out of him, more so than the fall did; or 2) he figured if he cries, he's likely to get a treat out of it, so he's going to milk his mother's distress for all its worth.

Well, I disagree. My little baby might really be hurt. I would be neglectful if I didn't express my concern or take him to the doctor. Or—you could educate yourself on childhood injuries and potentially save considerable money on emergency room fees. Children are going to fall down and get hurt. It's a fact of growing up. If they get a cut or a scrape then cleanse it, put antibiotic on it, and apply a Band-Aid. If they fall and bump their head, then watch for signs of concussion. According to the experts at the Mayo Clinic (2016), those signs, as it relates to infants and toddlers are:

"Head trauma is very common in young children. But concussions can be difficult to recognize in infants and toddlers because they may not be able to describe how they feel. Nonverbal clues of a concussion may include:

Appearing dazed

Listlessness and tiring easily

Irritability and crankiness

Loss of balance and unsteady walking

Crying excessively

Change in eating or sleeping patterns

Lack of interest in favorite toys

When to see a doctor

See a doctor within one to two days if:

You or your child experiences a head injury, even if emergency care isn't required

The American Academy of Pediatrics recommends that you call your child's doctor for advice if your child receives anything more than a light bump on the head.

If your child doesn't have signs of a serious head injury, and if your child remains alert, moves normally and responds to you, the injury is probably mild and usually doesn't need further testing. In this case, if your child wants to nap, it's OK to let him or her sleep. If worrisome signs develop later, seek emergency care.

Seek emergency care for an adult or child who experiences a head injury and symptoms such as:

Repeated vomiting

A loss of consciousness lasting longer than 30 seconds

A headache that gets worse over time

Changes in his or her behavior, such as irritability

Changes in physical coordination, such as stumbling or clumsiness

Confusion or disorientation, such as difficulty recognizing people or places

Slurred speech or other changes in speech

Other symptoms include:

Seizures

Vision or eye disturbances, such as pupils that are bigger than normal (dilated pupils) or pupils of unequal sizes

Lasting or recurrent dizziness

Obvious difficulty with mental function or physical coordination

Symptoms that worsen over time

Large head bumps or bruises on areas other than the forehead in children, especially in infants under 12 months of age

The hard part, when a child is hurt, is remaining calm, cool, and collected, so that we don't generate fear in our child. We are their rock, and if we crumble, they're going to crumble too.

Potty Training

Of all the areas in which parents have an abundance of stress, the biggest, next to disciplining, occurs when their child reaches that magical age where they will begin to learn to transition from peeing and pooing in a diaper to climbing up on a toilet like the big boys and girls they're becoming. Some parents want to start this the moment their child begins to walk in an effort to get it behind them as quickly as possible, so to stop paying through the nose for diapers or pull ups. Others opt to hold off until they're child makes the move on their own, automatically, sometimes waiting until their child is three-and-a-half or older. I've met, and worked with, both of these types of parents, and discovered something interesting: pushing your child too soon, or waiting too late, is going to elevate your stress levels to a whole new high.

I do have a recommendation, based on experience, but this is only a recommendation. One that I've had success with.

When your child advances in age far enough to be able to walk and to speak in a few sentences (generally around age two-and-a-half), their comprehension is also improving. In order to toilet train successfully, you need all three of these components in play: walking, speaking, and comprehension. Some children develop faster or slower than others, so age two-and-a-half is an estimation.

Prior to this, to set your child up for comprehending the purpose of a toilet, have them accompany you or your spouse to the restroom and sit on a potty seat. Around age two, transition them to pull-ups. Why? Because pull-ups hold less pee and also allows a child to feel the moisture against their skin, spurring discomfort and developing the want to not have that discomfort. Keep any leftover diapers for nighttime wear, to avoid accidents while your child is learning.

Next, work on timing and communication. Train your child to let you know when they "need to go". While they are learning this new skill, take them to the restroom, like clockwork, every hour to every hour and a half. Whether they go or not is irrelevant. You are training them and that takes time, consistency, and loads of patience. It will also train their bladder—a muscle—to hold urine a bit longer, getting stronger.

Earlier I made an analogy about getting upset with a dog for snatching food off a plate left lying around. Well, toilet training is very similar to training a new puppy. In order to prevent accidents, you must be consistent in the training. A puppy is actually a bit harder because they can't communicate.

Following consistent, repetitive, calm, and encouraging communication with your child will see them toilet trained within a month or so. I've had some get the idea within two weeks. Some may require six months. The key is calm, encouraging, consistent repetition: "If you need to go potty, let me know." (And don't get upset if they don't. This is new for them, so just keep repeating it). "Let's go potty now" (every hour to an hour-and-a-half). I have a specific question related to this topic that I'll address in the *Some additional questions I've been asked* section.

Educating yourself on childhood injuries, technology, and other areas of childhood development is one of the best methods to prevent fretting over EVERYTHING.

Conclusion

A wiser person than I once told me that I could ignore his advice or I could take it and apply it—my choice; however, if I sought out that advice, he was going to give it. That wise person was my father, and I sought his advice many times in my life. Some I applied some I chose to overlook. My choice. It's something I've carried over into my own dealings with my children and parents who've come to me with their questions—I don't offer unsolicited advice. However, if they ask, I'm going to give it to them. Whether they apply that advice is for them to decide.

I say that because, if you picked up this book and determined to read it, you are, in essence, seeking my advice; however, whether you apply that advice is up to you.

I'm not a know-it-all. I'm a parent; and it's been a rollercoaster ride of joy and pain. But I'm still standing, and my children are rather decent human beings, so as far as advice goes, you could do worse than applying mine.

Some of the scenarios and examples given in this text have been rather harsh, but life is harsh, making parenting today truly a challenge. If you and your spouse stand united, with knowledge in one hand, determination in the other, and the will to be the parents in your home—you'll be able to weather any storm; and your children will grow up with the same ability to weather any storm. Here's at least one person that has faith that the children of tomorrow can be strong, self-sufficient, responsible, caring adults—if their parents train them to be so today.

Some questions I've been asked

When is it okay to take a baby outside, in public, or allow them around people, after birth?

It's perfectly okay to take your child outside or to visit relatives as soon as the little one is born; however, there are some commonsense rules to follow:

1. Don't take them to a relative's home if you know there are sick people in attendance.

2. Avoid going where there are large crowds, because there will invariably be someone sick that could infect your child.

3. If your baby is sickly from the onset, discuss outings with your pediatrician in advance.

Here's some information on the subject by CNN reporter, Cynthia Cohn:

"While going out to crowded places is a bad idea, it's also a mistake to stay home 24-7 for six weeks with your newborn. Look at postpartum depression -- what could be more depressing than being cooped up with a kid who's not talking to you and cries all the time?" says Brown.

Brown encourages her patients to take their newborns for walks outside. She also tells them if they need to take the baby to the grocery store, to pick a time when it will be less crowded" (2007).

When should I take my child to the doctor?

This is a judgement call, and not for me to say; however, these are the rules I've followed when caring for my own children—none of which have suffered any ill effects from my decisions; and which has saved me considerable money.

1) If your baby/toddler/child has a fever that is one-hundred-two, get them to the doctor. Under that, try Tylenol and a room-temperature bath to lower the fever. If the fever keeps returning (or getting higher), get them to the doctor.

2) If your child has an inexplicable rash (not a diaper rash) and it can't be explained away as poison ivy/oak/sumac, irritation due to laundry detergent, allergic reaction, or resolved with a phone call to a nurse hotline, then take them to the doctor.

My daughter told me this, which she thought should be included:

"Kaitlyn had a major rash that we couldn't get rid of even with medicinal rash cream. Our daycare lady mentioned that it could have been caused by something I was eating or drinking. I had been drinking tons of water flavored with powder packs, to try to keep my milk production up. It was the citric acid in those packs that caused the major rash! Once I stopped using the packs and made sure I wasn't drinking anything with citric acid in it, even the smallest amount, her rash went away and once I stopped breastfeeding, I went back to my flavored water."

3) If your child falls down but has no more than a few scratches (no gaping wounds), then clean them up and let it be. They'll live. If they suffer a bump on the head, check for signs of concussion (I go more in depth on this in the section on *injuries*). If they have a gushing wound, bandage it, and take them in for stitches.

How often should I feed my newborn?

Newborns know when they are hungry, so you need to feed them when they start demanding it. It generally ranges from every hour at birth, decreasing in time as they get older. Of course, this is all dependent up many factors: Some children are heavier eaters than others, requiring feeding more often; and some moms produce too little milk to satiate a baby, requiring more frequent nursing, or supplementing with formula.

"A baby is smarter than any grown-up," says Dr. Robin Madden, a pediatrician in Silver Spring, Maryland. "Whether breast-fed or bottle-fed, they know when they're hungry and they know when they're full. Babies don't feed on a cookie-cutter pattern. If you follow their demand, they're going to eat better". (11)

When do I start correcting/disciplining?

I cover this beneath infants section but am summarizing it here because it's asked of me quite a bit. Newborns to between five-eight months are innocent of behaviors that require correction. After that, verbalizing appropriate behaviors in a positive manner, and using a stern tone to correct negative behaviors is sufficient. No longer may a parent smack a child's hand or smack their bottoms. Doing so today will cause someone to report you to CPS (Child Protective Services). The good news is, though, that if you follow the disciplinary template provided—time out, discuss, consequence—you won't need to spank.

Is baby talk counterproductive?

Not really, no. However, with that being said, I never used it, preferring to speak to my children in a manner that I would use throughout their lives. Personally, I think this is better in that it instructs children from the onset how proper words are used in proper context, which to me can only be beneficial.

What if my baby isn't developing as fast as they should (walking, talking, etc)?

Stop fretting over this so much. Babies are going to develop differently at different times. Although there are "guidelines" as to gauging a baby's progress, these are merely guidelines. There is nothing wrong with your baby if they start walking at fifteen months or if they decide to wait until they are twenty-four months. I've worked with babies who took forever to develop, and they turned out just fine; and I've worked with those who develop superfast—also fine. With that being said—if your child reaches one year of age and is not making lots of noise or starting to form simple words by approximately two years; if they are still crawling but have made no attempts at standing or walking—that's when I'd consult your pediatrician.

If I want my baby to have a playmate (I want another child), what should the age gap be?

This is another judgement call. My first two were born nearly a year apart—nearly to the day. While my second two have a gap of two-and-a-half years. Based on those criteria, I would prefer that both have been apart approximately one-and-a-half years. This gives the eldest time enough to comprehend the meaning of "a new brother or sister", yet still be young enough, as they age, to enjoy each other's company. If too far apart (as with my second two), jealousy develops because the youngest wants to do that which the oldest gets to do (like learn to drive, date, etc.). Also, if too far apart, the older may revert to being an "infant" in order to return to getting momma and daddy's attention as the newborn is getting. This may result in toilet using reversal, where the elder begins to use the bathroom in his or her pants again because that's what the youngest gets to do. If one-and-a-half years, the oldest is still *in* diapers, solving that issue readily. Again, this is my opinion based on experience.

How do we prevent parental imbalance?

This question is referring to those instances when one parent seems to be favored by a child over the other parent. This is generally a result of one being the sole disciplinarian while the other is the "playmate". Remember at the beginning of the book when I said that parents needed to present a united front? Well, this is part of that topic. Parents need to "discipline" together as well as be a child's "playmate" together. There can be no imbalance, or the child will divide and conquer.

How should I react if my child has a bathroom accident after being toilet trained?

Calmly. After bathing the child, discuss the importance of using the toilet as a big boy or girl should. Most times, using the bathroom in the pants has an underlying cause: 1) was the bathroom too far away, 2) is there a newborn in the house; 3) was there a stressor (fear)? Whatever the cause, it needs to be addressed as calmly as if toilet training for the first time.

How do I deal with people telling me how to raise my child?

You mean like I'm doing?

Take the advice or leave it, but with an understanding that everyone has got an opinion they want to share. Don't take offense. After all, you're still the one going to raise your child, not them. If your mother-in-law is convinced she knows what's best, let her talk (but not in front of the little ones, especially if she's prone to being critical of you); give her a kiss on the cheek, and thank her. If it's your friend who's raised a few—listen politely (out of earshot of the kids), thank her, and then continue raising your child your way. If it's a stranger—tell them to mind their own business because they don't have any business meddling in a stranger's affairs. Yes, I'm serious.

Now—why did I keep writing "out of earshot of the kids"? Because, just as you and your spouse need to be on the same page and present a united front, so should your friends and family appear to be in agreement with everything you do and say. If they undermine your authority in front of your children, it's going to make you appear weak and easily conquered; so, if your friend or family member has two cents to add, pull them aside, out of earshot of the children, and then let them have their say. In any case, don't get upset. It's not worth the gray hairs and wrinkles.

One of my children is more frustrating than the other. How do I deal with that?

First of all you need to realize that all children will have different personalities. Some may come off like a Mother Theresa and the other like Satan in the flesh; however, IF you parent each consistently with the same template discussed in this book (time out, discussion, consequence); and reward consistently also, then the differences won't matter, and your children won't feel as if one is preferred over the other (which is where some of these extreme differences in personality originate).

Is there something to homemade remedies?

Use caution unless they've been proven. Homemade remedies can be just as harmful as any medications if untested and administered improperly. If you have questions, ask a physician.

Can showering a child with gifts be balanced with teaching them hard work and earning things?

My philosophy on this is the same as that which I discussed related to money (You're not the bank). I think that gifts are great—when the occasion calls for it—birthdays or holidays; and an occasional "just because I love you". However, I do not think that "showering" a child with gifts continually is wise because it creates a "demand" or "expectation" within that child, a sense of entitlement. For instance—if you have a habit of buying your child a toy every time you go shopping, then you're developing that expectation within your child who will soon demand that toy when you go shopping, even if you cannot afford it. Also, by "giving" too much, your child will not learn to value "earning" something by working for it. If your child earns something by working for it, then they can't be "showered" too much, because they will view what you give as something earned, not something they're entitled to.

At what age should I allow a child to have a "pet of their own"? Should I give it away if they don't care for it?

First, no pet will ever belong to a single member of a family. Even if a pet is given to a child as a birthday present (my third child got a kitten for her fourth birthday and is still with us today, loved and tended to by all), that pet will quickly become a member of the family; community property. If it's a turtle or a fish that cohabitates with a specific child, that may be different, but a child is incapable of caring sufficiently for an animal on their own until they are a teen or adult and should be supervised by a parent consistently until then. Why? Well, let's look at it this way—if a child is incapable of tending to their own needs (cooking for themselves, washing their own clothes, etc.) how can they possibly be expected to tend to another living animal? So, if you plan to allow a child a "pet of their own", then you better make certain that you are going to be ready, willing, and able to tend to that pet also—even if in a supervisory capacity. Otherwise, forgo until they're a teen.

Should it be given away if not cared for? Yes. Why? Because if the parent is too busy to supervise, then that household is not ready for a pet—and it won't be the child's fault.

How much time should I set aside for my child? I have a million and one things that I have to do each day?

There's an old saying—it isn't the quantity, rather the quality that matters. That's true with time spent with children also. Some parents go overboard, dedicating so much time to a child that when they finally realize that they don't have that much time every day…well, the child doesn't accept that and starts the temper tantrums to get that time back. The same will happen for a child who is ignored frequently or regularly—temper tantrums ensue to get attention. It all comes down to balance.

If your child sees how hard you work, that's a good example for them—especially if you also take a half hour, an hour, or two hours out of your day (whatever's feasible), to spend *quality* time with them—whether you're watching a movie together, going to the park, having a family outing, or helping with homework. If you dedicate a time each day to spend with your child, then they will appreciate you all the more and will be less likely to become demanding of your time.

Why does my baby cry when someone else holds him?

Your baby is simply unfamiliar with the smell; or the smell of the person may be unpleasant. Either way, don't force your baby into that person's company. Eventually, they'll get used to whomever it is and approach on their own. Forcing them will cause unneeded distress. It took two years for my daughters to get near their grandmother and it had nothing to do with her. There was simply something they weren't ready to accept. Once they realized who she was, they made the move on their own. It helped that my mom and I were in agreement on allowing them time.

What time should my baby/toddler/child be put to bed?

Knowing this is directly related to what time they get up each day.

According to the National Sleep Foundation (2016), here's how to determine a bedtime:

1) Infants need between twelve-fifteen hours of sleep.

2) Toddlers need between eleven-to-fourteen hours of sleep.

3) Ages three-five need between ten-thirteen hours of sleep.

4) Ages six-thirteen need between nine-to-eleven hours of sleep.

5) Ages fourteen-seventeen need between eight-to-ten hours of sleep.

So, if their wake-up time is at six a.m., then subtract the recommended number of sleep hours to get their bedtime. Example: A toddler rises at six a.m. and requires approximately twelve hours of sleep. That means that they need to go to bed at six p.m. (Sounds blissful for new parents wanting a few hours of peace and alone time, doesn't it?).

How can I encourage my son to talk about school when he's not much a communicator?

Ask questions that do not require a simple "yes" or "no" response. Instead of asking, "Did you have a nice day at school?" try instead, "Tell me one new thing you learned today" or "What was one thing you learned in science?" If they try the "I don't know" ploy, keep asking questions until they "do know" something. If you start this young enough, it will simply become a habit and it will teach your child how to communicate.

A specific question related to section: *If you don't know the answer say "Let's look it up": How would "I don't know the answer" or "Let's look it up" work related to pray time? We pray with our children and somewhat openly pray for friends, family and sometimes our own issues. Would it be more in regards to keeping it less detailed or being rather generalized and be more specific when we pray alone?*

Praying is a different method of communicating. When we communicate with our children, we want them to trust us and to ensure they come to us for answers; we want to develop a "superhero" mentality within them, so they seek our wisdom and not someone else's.

When we pray to our heavenly Father, it's something different altogether. We're not expressing our ignorance in front of our children, rather we are teaching our children how to speak to their heavenly Father: to grant peace, to help heal the sick, to assist in finances…whatever the subject matter, it has nothing to do with how our children view us—the parents.

Several questions related to section: *Toddler "Playtime"*:

How does "sharing" work if a child comes over to my house? If he leaves his toys at home, comes over to play with my child's toy? How can you say 'this toy is not to be shared' thing you said?

To prevent "sharing" a toy when children come over to your home to play simply don't take it out; or place it atop the closet. If you know that your son or daughter just received a new toy that they want to keep for themselves for a while, put it away when children come over to play. Then you don't need to worry over "sharing" that toy.

If your child has an issue sharing *any* of his or her toys, you have one or two options: 1) don't invite children over to play; or 2) select group toys for playtime and then let your son or daughter know that they will need to share these during their play date. Avoid putting out toys that can only be played with by a single child.

What if my kid goes to his friend's house (who has lots of 'new' toys he doesn't like to share) but still expects my son to play with him?

Going to someone else's home means having to contend with their rules, which can be trying when those rules counter your own. If it is a really huge issue which creates continual upset, you have a few options: 1) stop going to that house and select a neutral territory for play dates (i.e. a local park), 2) if they insist on making the play date at their home, have your son take a toy that he can play with and/or can share with his friend, 3) ask the parent how she would resolve the issue. See if you can find a resolution together.

How do you handle a situation where a kid pitches a fit over a toy he wasn't even playing with, but another child is playing with it; or a child who hoards toys?

I've had this happen—both types—with children from a single-child home who've joined our daycare family. They don't have to share at home because everything is theirs. So, when they want a toy, they think it's okay to simply take it from another child; or they will say, "No! Mine!" and snatch it away; or they will tuck all of the toys in a corner, or under a chair…

Eyes get round as saucers the first time I tell them, in response to the fit-pitching, or "no, it's mine" outburst, or the hoarding: "Those belong to Mrs. Barbara, and if we can share it, we will. If we can't, then you'll need to wait until it's available to play with. In either case, it isn't appropriate for you to snatch toys from other children, or hide toys, so we're not going to do that again. Now return all of the toys to the play area so that all can enjoy them."

Dealing with that during a play date is not much different. Calmly explain that toys are meant to be played with and if it can be played with by more than one person, it will be. If not, then they will have to be patient and play with something else until the toy comes available. Remember to avoid permissive phrases: "Don't you want to share?" "Don't you think it would be nice to let Timmy play with your GI Joe?" "Do you want to share your dinosaur collection?" Permissive phrases set children up to make the decision and they already are of the mindset that they don't want to share.

A specific question related to the section: *Potty Training*

This particular question is multi-faceted, so I'll try to break it down into answerable segments:

What if your child gets used to the routine of the hour/hour and a half and won't go to the toilet until he hears that 'buzzer' saying it's a potty break, yet still has accidents as early as thirty minutes or forty-five minutes prior?

The intent behind taking a child on a schedule is to train and strengthen the muscles in the urinary and excretory systems. Until going becomes routine, and the muscles are strong enough to "hold it" for a short stint, then there are going to be accidents. Pull ups are expensive, but until the habit is formed again, it may be a good idea to go back to using them.

Patience and perseverance will ensure that the parent stays calm during those "accidents". Routine and consistency will ensure that the child gets the idea and will start to use the toilet instead of having accidents in his pants.

Setbacks *will* occur and getting angry or frustrated at your child will generate insecurity and fear within that child that will cause more accidents to occur; so it is absolutely imperative you remain calm and work with the child until they learn what needs to take place and where.

How do you contain frustration when you've left a store with a restroom, climb into the car and start driving, only to have your child pipe up that they have to go?

First, when children are distracted, they aren't thinking of having to go to the restroom, and there are going to be distractions when shopping. Second, they may not have had to go in the store. This was something that I learned to accept with my own children—they don't necessarily have to go when you say, "We're in the store with a restroom. Go pee before we head to the car." Well, just because we say to do it, doesn't mean they need to. Also, a car's movement can generate a need to go in some children. In the end, the only thing you can do is pull over at a local McDonalds and run them to the restroom. And I'll repeat it again—remaining calm will help them. If you're always frustrated and angry over their mishaps, they are going to have more accidents and they aren't going to want to verbalize when they need to go (communication breaks down or becomes nonexistent).

There was a girl in my daycare who would duck beside something (the chair or the kitchen play set) when she was going poo, because she didn't want to tell me she had to go. Why do you think she did that? I found out it was because her mom would yell at her when she had an accident or when she wouldn't go on the toilet when her mom put her there. Remember, taking a child to the toilet is a training tool meant to show them where to go and how. During this time, they won't always need to go.

How do you deal with potty training when you're trying one way and the other parent is making it difficult and getting frustrated?

As with all areas of parenting, there needs to be a consensus between the parents on how they will deal with issues that arise. If a child starts going to the restroom in his pants, the parents need to immediately sit down and discuss their strategy so one parent isn't making the child feel "bad", which will counter any effort made by the parent working calmly to correct the issue. The parents must be on the same page. As I mentioned earlier, you won't be able to formulate a plan for every scenario that will occur prior to the birth of a child; however, you can sit down and calmly discuss what y'all will do as a couple to rectify issues as they arise. The key, however, will always be unity, patience, consistency, and perseverance.

It's very frustrating because he has no problem going pee, but if I tell him to sit on the toilet he can't stand it and even fusses/pitches a fit, especially if he had an accident. Even when I tell him I'm not mad at him, but I will be if he keeps that fussiness up. What are we doing so wrong?

Your son probably already has a negative view of the toilet, which is why he's pitching a fit. I would stop making him sit on the toilet, as the accident has already occurred and making him sit on the toilet after the fact is a punishment in his eyes. This is compounding his already negative view of the toilet.

Clean him up and simply tell him, "Okay, we'll try it again in a little while. No worries, we'll get it right." Then let it go.

Don't harp on it or punish him for it. This is one area where punishing will backfire, because he isn't in control of his bowels and generating fear or anger will make it harder to learn to control his bowels. If you keep up the routine—"Let's head to the toilet now", eventually his system will strengthen and he won't have accidents; eventually it will mesh in his brain that that's where he needs to do his business.

Parenting Styles

Written by Kendra Cherry, Reviewed by Steven Gans, M.D. on VeryWellMind website, 2/2018

Authoritarian Parenting

One of the three major styles identified by Baumrind was the authoritarian style. In this style of parenting, children are expected to follow the strict rules established by the parents. Failure to follow such rules usually results in punishment. Authoritarian parents don't explain the reasoning behind these rules. If asked to explain, the parent might simply reply, "Because I said so."

While these parents have high demands, they are not very responsive to their children. They expect their children to behave exceptionally and not make errors, yet they provide very little direction about what their children should do or avoid in the future. Mistakes are punished, often quite harshly, yet their children are often left wondering exactly what they did wrong.

According to Baumrind, these parents "are obedience- and status-oriented, and expect their orders to be obeyed without explanation."

Parents who exhibit this style are often described as domineering and dictatorial. Their approach to parenting is one of "spare the rod, spoil the child." Despite having such strict rules and high expectations, they do little to explain the reasoning behind their demands and simply expect children to obey without question.

Authoritative Parenting

A second major style identified by Baumrind was the authoritative style. Like authoritarian parents, those with an authoritative parenting style establish rules and guidelines that their children are expected to follow. However, this parenting style is much more democratic.

Authoritative parents are responsive to their children and willing to listen to questions. These parents expect a lot of their children, but they provide warmth, feedback, and adequate support.

When children fail to meet the expectations, these parents are more nurturing and forgiving rather than punishing.

Baumrind suggested that these parents "monitor and impart clear standards for their children's conduct. They are assertive, but not intrusive and restrictive. Their disciplinary methods are supportive, rather than punitive. They want their children to be assertive as well as socially responsible, and self-regulated as well as cooperative."

It is this combination of expectation and support that helps children of authoritative parents develop skills such as independence, self-control, and self-regulation.

Permissive Parenting

The final style identified by Baumrind was what is known as the permissive style of parenting. Permissive parents sometimes referred to as indulgent parents, have very few demands to make of their children. These parents rarely discipline their children because they have relatively low expectations of maturity and self-control.

According to Baumrind, permissive parents "are more responsive than they are demanding. They are nontraditional and lenient, do not require mature behavior, allow considerable self-regulation, and avoid confrontation."

Permissive parents are generally nurturing and communicative with their children, often taking on the status of a friend more than that of a parent.

Uninvolved Parenting

In addition to the three major styles introduced by Baumrind, psychologist Eleanor Maccoby and John Martin proposed a fourth style that is known as uninvolved or neglectful parenting. An uninvolved parenting style is characterized by few demands, low responsiveness, and very little communication.

While these parents fulfill the child's basic needs, they are generally detached from their child's life. They might make sure that their kids are fed and have shelter, but offer little to nothing in the way of guidance, structure, rules, or even support. In extreme cases, these parents may even reject or neglect the needs of their children.

Ask the Author

If I missed a topic you still have questions about, you're more than welcome to email it to me and I'll gladly reply. Please note however, that any questions received may be used in future works related to parenting.

Email me at:

Barb97223@gmail.com

About the author

I live in Oregon with my husband, Tim, and my two youngest daughters. The remaining five children are scattered across the globe, but—thanks to technology—we are never more than a message or call away.

As stated in the introduction, I'm a business owner. I'm also an educator and a published author. Prior to this book, all my works have been in the fiction category. If interested in learning more, information can be located at www.LiteraryAdventures.net

FOOTNOTES:

(1) Pupil definition: Merriam-Webster Dictionary online

(2) definition of self-flagellation: Merriam-Webster Dictionary online

(3) definition of discipline: Cambridge.org

(4) Raisingchildren.net

(5) McDermott, 2014

(6) Ogden, 2011

(7) Healthline.com, 2015

(8) Dodge & Hergman, 2010

(9) Narvaez, 2011

(10) Stores, 2016

(11) Cohn, 2007

References

Atkins, R. (2006). Watching You. [Album: Going through Hell]. Produced by Curb Records.

Baumrind, D. Child-care practices anteceding three patterns of preschool behavior. Genetic Psychology Monographs. 1967; 75: 43-88.

Benson, JB, Marshall, MH. Social and Emotional Development in Infancy and Early Childhood. Oxford: Academic Press; 2009.

Cherry, K. Why parenting styles matter when raising children. Retrieved from https://www.verywellmind.com/parenting-styles-2795072

Cohn, C. (2007). 5 mistakes parents make with newborns—and how to avoid them. Retrieved from http://www.cnn.com/2007/HEALTH/family/09/05/ep.newborn.mistakes/index.html?cref=rss_health

Dodge, D., & Heroman, C. (2010). Building your baby's brain. Washington, D.C.: Teaching Strategies.

Huh, D, Tristan, J, Wade, E & Stice, E Does Problem Behavior Elicit Poor Parenting?: A Prospective Study of Adolescent Girls. Journal of Adolescent Research. 2006; 21(2): 185-204.

Macklem, GL. Practitioner's Guide to Emotion Regulation in School-Aged Children. New York: Springer; 2008.

McDermott, M. (2014). 10 Facts About How Our Brain Gets Angry. Retrieved from http://tvblogs.nationalgeographic.com/2014/08/15/10-facts-about-how-our-brain-gets-angry/

Narvaez, D. (2011). Dangers of "crying it out". Retrieved from https://www.psychologytoday.com/blog/moral-landscapes/201112/dangers-crying-it-out

National Sleep Foundation. (2016). Retrieved from https://sleepfoundation.org/excessivesleepiness/sleep-news/how-much-sleep-do-babies-and-kids-need

Ogden, J. (2011). Brilliant, Brazen, Teenage Brains. Retrieved from https://www.psychologytoday.com/blog/trouble-in-mind/201112/brilliant-brazen-teenage-brains

Raisingchildren.net.au,. (2010). Staying positive—tips for parents | Raising Children Network. Retrieved from http://raisingchildren.net.au/articles/positive_attention.html

The signs of concussion in infants and toddlers. (2016). The Mayo Clinic. Retrieved from http://www.mayoclinic.org/diseases-conditions/concussion/basics/symptoms/con-20019272

Smith, G. & Cerny, D. (2008). Why so many allergies—now? Retrieved from http://allergicliving.com/2010/11/20/allergies-why-so-many-now/

Storrs, C. (2016). It's okay to let your baby cry himself to sleep, studies find. Retrieved from http://www.cnn.com/2016/05/24/health/cry-it-out-sleep-training-ok/

Thompson, P. (n.d.). Judgement last to develop [image]. Retrieved from GoogleImages.com

www.ingramcontent.com/pod-product-compliance
Lightning Source LLC
Chambersburg PA
CBHW052050070526
44584CB00017B/2119